BLACKOUT:

My 40 Years in the Music Business

Paul Porter

with Reva G. Harris and Lauren Carter

Published by BookLocker.com, Inc., St. Petersburg, Florida, U.S.A.

Printed on acid-free paper.

This is a work of nonfiction. Some names and other identifying characteristics have been changed to protect the privacy and anonymity of the individuals involved.

BookLocker.com, Inc.
2017

First Edition

I dedicate this book to my beloved mother, Lillian Amoy Porter.

Brandy Walker-Arrajj, I am so thankful for your unconditional love and support.

CONTENTS

Introduction

Do you know Karen Kline? I do. And so do a lot of people in the music industry. She used to be a good friend of mine. For a minute, I was in love with her, even though I knew the relationship could never last. Karen's known and loved throughout the world of music, video and radio. And she has this *incredible* ability to be in many different places at the *exact* same time.

I met Karen while I was staying at the Hotel George in Washington, D.C. It was 1999, and I had just been hired as the Program Director at BET, the fast-growing entertainment channel that was being broadcast into more than 48 million homes. My job would be deciding what videos to play on the channel.

By this time, music videos had surpassed radio as the place to break a record. And my friends at the major record labels were not going to take any chances. One weekend, a FedEx truck pulled up to the Hotel George with two packages for me. Both packages were exactly the same; there were $5,000 dollars in each, wrapped tightly in plastic. No return address, no instructions, just the name "Karen Kline," a fictional woman I loved like she was flesh and blood.

It's called payola. And it's as old as recorded music itself. Even the word itself tells you how far it goes back. Payola is a contraction between the words "pay" and "Victrola," the old-school phonograph that was used to spin the very first records.

Payola is firmly embedded in the music industry, deep in the grooves like tracks on a vinyl record. It's been going on for so long that it's hard to believe that people are still getting away with it. But they are. I know I did. And my relationship with Karen Kline was a one-night stand compared to how she's operating today.

Karen Kline is not just visiting people on Saturday mornings anymore. She's married — to corporate America. And she's bringing in more money than anyone could ever fit inside a FedEx envelope.

Chapter 1: I Got the Message

You never know what the day will bring. I stood tall as I stared at the note the little girl handed to me. It read:

"Dear Mr. Paul, I know you work at HOT 97 and KISS, and I want to know if you can get that Rah Digga song, 'beat that bitch with a bat' off the radio? Why do they play songs like that?"

Lea was a quiet girl who attended P.S. 192 in Queens, N.Y. It was the same school that Jam Master Jay of Run-D.M.C. had attended many years before. I volunteered there twice a week, speaking to kids about the communications industry, and I knew most of the kids in the school.

"They keep playing that song on the radio," Lea said. "You know that really happened to my mother. You just don't understand, Mr. Paul. My mom is in the hospital. My father beat her with a bat, and all the kids are teasing me."

I was beginning to understand. Every time she heard that song, it took her back to that horrible image of her mother being beaten. Up to that point in my life, I'd always had an answer, even if it was bullshit, but I found myself at a loss for words before this young girl.

I thought about the promotions that were running on HOT 97. They were excerpts from a contest that DJ Sway aired on his morning show. He asked a third-grade student to name the first black president; the child paused and then answered "Bill Clinton." Then Sway asked how many times the rapper 50 Cent had been shot. The child replied immediately with the correct answer, and then the voice-over announced: "Who says HOT 97 doesn't teach young children?"

By the time I met Lea at P.S. 192, I'd had enough. I could no longer ignore the negative lyrics and derogatory stereotypes that pervaded black music. When I read her carefully worded note, I knew I wasn't going to just let it go.

I heard Rah Digga's song "Party & Bullshit" on the morning drive every day. It was an urban anthem. Although I never played "Party & Bullshit" on KISS, where I worked as a part-time announcer, it aired on our sister station, HOT 97. I thought about that line, *"I beat that bitch with a bat (Say what?!)."* I looked at Lea's note again. Then, I looked at Lea and said, "I'm going to see what I can do. I'll get back to you in a few days with an answer."

I made good on my word. When I went back to the corporate office, I wrote an email to Barry Mayo, Senior Vice President for Emmis Radio-New York — which included HOT 97, KISS-FM, and CD 101.9 — and to Tracy Cloherty, who was the Program Director for HOT 97. I told everyone who would listen that we were not going to play "Party & Bullshit" or any other song with negative lyrics. As a well-respected veteran in the music industry, I figured I was in a position to do something positive. It had taken more than 27 years of hard work to get to this level, and I was going to use my power to make a difference.

After a few days with no response, I sent the email to Barry and Tracy again, and again got no response. Over the course of two weeks, I reached out at least four times, but I never received a response from either of them.

Finally, Barry responded verbally. "Man what are you doing? You're going to have to choose what you want to do," he said. "Don't complain. These songs are part of the format. Why do you want to stop this record? Make up your mind. Do you want to stand up for kids or the company?"

He boasted to me about giving money to poor people in the 'hoods. I told him that it didn't make any difference what we gave, if with the other hand we devalued every good deed with negative messages. I wrote another email to Barry to document the conversation. I copied Toya Beasley, who was the Program Director at KISS-FM.

My next step was to write Jeffrey Smulyan, CEO and Founder of Emmis Communications. He was located somewhere at corporate headquarters in Indianapolis. His company owned seven or eight stations across the country. Jeff, whom I had never met, answered my email. He expressed shock and surprise that the station was playing those types of lyrics; he said there was no way a record with lines like "I'll beat that bitch with a bat" should have been on at the times it was being played. He told me he would look into it and that it would be taken care of.

HOT 97 immediately pulled "Party & Bullshit" off the air, along with a lot of other songs filled with derogatory lyrics. Two days later, I came into the station at midnight for my overnight shift. Across the hallway, I could see Funkmaster Flex getting off the air and Fatman Scoop preparing to go on. Fatman Scoop called me into the studio.

"You're famous," he said, pointing to a memo on the wall from Tracy Cloherty stating that all hip-hop mixes must be clean and free of profanity.

When I saw that memo posted inside the studio, I felt a rush of pride. It was a small feat and a small victory, but it meant the world to me. There was no way I could erase all of the mistakes I'd made. But slowly, I could try to make things better. I looked more closely at the memo. At the bottom of it, someone had handwritten: *Thank Paul Porter from Kiss-FM for this.* By the time I saw the memo, it had already been posted for two days.

I debated the issue with Fatman Scoop. He wanted to know why I would contact Jeff Smulyan. I told him that it was the right thing to do. Fatman Scoop told me that HOT 97 needed an extra edge — they wanted to be a harder station than New York rival Power 105.1. I told him that airing songs with profanity and violent lyrics was not the way to have an edge. He told me that he made sure to "school" his kids about what they heard on the radio. I told him that was great, but not every kid has a dad to filter what's heard on radio or seen on television. He understood.

In the end, I recall only Fatman Scoop supporting my position. The rest of the staff acted as though something was wrong with me. I was a whistleblower. One young DJ approached me and said, "Man you don't know what you're talking about. That record is happening in the streets." According to him, I was just an old man who was out of touch. Nevertheless, the airwaves were clean at HOT 97 for one full week.

Then Toya Beasley, the Program Director at KISS, called me up, wanting to know what was going on. She was nervous. She said Barry Mayo and Tracy Cloherty were upset about one of the jocks who worked for her. I told her the whole story, and she said she believed in everything I was saying, but HOT 97 wasn't her station and she couldn't control what went on over there. She told me I needed to talk to Barry Mayo.

I did call Barry; and he was angry. "You have to decide what you want to do," Barry said. "Do you want to work in radio or fight against it? You should have never gone over my head."

I reminded him that I tried to contact him four times and he didn't respond. I told him that I thought the promotions were inappropriate and ignorant. He responded by saying that I had no sense of humor. Barry and I continued arguing, and I told him that since the song "Party & Bullshit" was taken off the air, I must have been right. He told me there was no proof that the station had done anything wrong by playing the song. I told him the proof was in the little girl's note. In the middle of the conversation, Barry told me he needed to go, and then he hung up. For the next three weeks, my name wasn't on the schedule. I asked Toya Beasley what was up and she said to talk to Barry. I emailed Jeff Smulyan again, who also told me to talk to Barry.

Barry was upset that I had gone over his head, so I was "unofficially" suspended. I went home thinking I would be back on the air in a few weeks.

While I was waiting to be called back to work, I appeared on "It's Your Call with Lynn Doyle," a news show on a Comcast cable channel that airs from Maine to Maryland. The topic was Howard Stern and decency in broadcasting. I decided to change the topic and began talking about songs that were *not* being labeled indecent. When I started telling the host about Lil Jon's song "Get Low" and what the word "skeet" meant, her jaw dropped. The next day, I got a call from Jim Greenwood, a Congressman from Pennsylvania who appeared on the show with me. He was working on a bill to increase fines for indecency and wanted me to know that he agreed with the things I'd said.

The people in New York-area radio, however, did not agree. I saw Fred "Bugsy" Buggs after the show aired. He told me that I'd made a bad move.

"You always trying to be a hero," he said. "That's why you're not working."

But I didn't care what Bugsy thought. I'd never felt like I'd done anything more *right* than the moment I saw that memo on the walls of HOT 97. I was being punished for speaking out. I was not surprised.

When my mother found out what had happened, she went off on me: "Oh my God! Paul, what did you do? This is your job! How are you going to work at that job again?" I explained that this issue was bigger than my job. But my mother was old school. Her career advice was to shut your mouth and do what you were told. "Paul, Paul, dammit, Paul!" she exclaimed in a thick Trinidadian accent. She didn't know that this was serious business for me. It was my newfound passion. I had a soul, and I wanted to keep it. I had said it before when I worked at BET: "Morality is not negotiable." I had to live the talk.

By this time, my mother had already sold my childhood home in Queens and had relocated to Florida. I'd moved with my then-girlfriend out on Long Island for what was supposed to be a temporary situation. I had no savings or investments, and I was depressed. It didn't take long for my girl to find out that I was unemployed. She kicked me out of her house, and I was officially homeless.

I ended up sleeping at the radio station for four nights in a row. Even though I wasn't on the schedule, I had a key card that still worked, and the station was known for having folks sleeping on the various couches at the station. No one noticed me. After four nights

5

there, I spent two nights sleeping on the F Train before I finally went back to Long Island.

I had too much pride to ask my girlfriend to let me back in. So I went into her backyard and slept on the brick steps leading to her back porch, using my coat as a pillow. I felt like I'd hit rock bottom. I couldn't help but wonder if it was just a coincidence that this was happening to me at the same time I'd decided to do what was right when it came to decency in radio. Barry Mayo had asked me to make a choice. I could stay in radio or fight against it. I had never been one to accept the easy choices given to me. I always believed I could make my own way. I was determined to find a way to use the media to fight the media.

It was now obvious to me and to others that I wasn't going to be working at KISS-FM. I wasn't going to kiss ass to get a shift, so I knew I would have to make moves. While my key card was still working, I spent late nights at the station looking up job opportunities in Atlanta. I had friends and family there, and I thought it would be a good place for me to go to chill out and get my thoughts together.

I stopped through D.C. to visit friends, before moving to Atlanta. I started filling in at WAOK, a talk radio station in Atlanta that gave me the opportunity to speak out about the indecency in radio and video. I did a morning show called "CrossTalk" from 6 a.m. to 10 a.m. just to get some exposure. The station had several people on the air at night attempting to do the same thing — working for free just for the experience. I was starting from scratch, but I thought moving to talk radio would help me give a voice and put me in a position where I could make a difference.

WAOK was owned by CBS Radio, which also owns V-103. Whenever I sat in the booth at WAOK, I could see across the hall to V-103, and every morning, I'd see Frank Ski doing a morning show. Back in D.C., Frank Ski used to spin at the clubs. Now, he was making $400,000 a year doing a morning show. It really put a lot of things in perspective for me. My life in the entertainment industry had taken many twists and turns. I never imagined that I would be filling in — for free — on a talk radio show. But I couldn't dwell on how things had gone down. Coming to Atlanta was a new beginning for me, and I was happy to be there. I was doing radio that mattered, and I was able to see changes being made, big and small.

I had no idea that my plan to use the media to take over the media would happen as quickly as it did. I created the site IndustryEars.com because I noticed a steady downward spiral in hip-hop content, and I thought there was a need to discuss and attempt to correct the mess that was dominating airwaves and TV stations. The day after my site launched, I was on the air at WAOK with Jean Ross, discussing the latest fiasco: HOT 97 was sponsoring the "Smackfest" contest, in which contestants took turns smacking each other — live in the studio — in exchange for concert tickets.

I urged my listeners in Atlanta to visit the HOT 97 website, which was airing video footage of "Smackfest," and take action in response to this ridiculous, dangerous and pathetic promotional tool. I thought about what Barry Mayo had told me when I complained about the station's responsibility to young people. He said that I had no sense of humor. It turned out that in Atlanta, my listeners were just as humorless when they saw footage of the contest.

One of my listeners, a man named Dwayne Brown, sent an email to just about everyone at Emmis Communications and copied the U.S. Federal Communications Commission (FCC) and members of Congress. Mr. Brown pointed out the demographics that HOT 97 catered to and explained his feelings about the content the station was promoting. That very same day, the footage was taken off the website and the contest was taken off the air. I still had a few people that I stayed in touch with at HOT 97. I put in a call and it was confirmed: Dwayne Brown's letter had forced "Smackfest" out of business.

HOT 97 was already in trouble because of their parody of "We Are The World." In the wake of the tsunami that hit Southeast Asia, the morning show produced and performed a song mocking the event, which Dwayne Brown mentioned in his letter. The song became a national outrage. And while trying to deal with protests from the Asian community, the "Smackfest" contest seemed to underscore how tasteless and tactless the station could be.

I brought Dwayne Brown on my show the next day and read his email on the air. I was so excited to see that it could be done — one person could turn the tides at a massive corporation. I'd influenced Dwayne Brown to get an offensive promotion off the air.

A reporter from the *New York Post* Philip Recchia interviewed me and wrote a story about the incidents at HOT 97. The *New York Post* article came out on March 6, the day after my mother's birthday:

D.J. IN HOT 97 BAT-TLE
By PHILIP RECCHIA

An on-air personality at one of Hot 97's sister stations says he was booted off the air after complaining about a song that features the lyric "Beat that bitch with a bat." Paul Porter said his falling-out with KISS-FM came after being told by the embattled hip-hop outlet, "Make up your mind: Do you want to stand up for kids or the company?" The freelance announcer, who is also a volunteer instructor at a public school in Queens, told The Post that he voiced his concern last year after a 12-year-old student asked him, "Why does Hot 97 play these records?"

The offending song, "Party and Bulls- - -" by rap artist Rah Digger, was a favorite of the little girl's father who had recently beaten her mother, Porter said.

"I was shocked that a sixth-grader was so aware, but saddened that I had no answer," said Porter.

Although the announcer's complaint led to a new zero-tolerance policy for on-air profanity, Hot 97 just five months later launched a violent on-air contest called "Smackfest." That's where young women compete for a $500 prize by striking one another in the face, not only to try and produce the loudest slap but do the most physical damage including drawing blood. These revelations come less than a week after an associate of rapper The Game was shot outside Hot 97's

Manhattan studio by a man believed to be an associate of rival rapper 50 Cent, while "Fitty" was inside promoting his new album. 50 Cent had just said on the air that he was ejecting The Game, a former protégé, from his posse.

Six weeks earlier, the station came under fire for playing "The Tsunami Song," a twisted "We Are the World" parody mocking victims of the natural disaster that killed more than 200,000 people. Porter says the Hot 97 DJs told him soon after the shooting that the controversies stem from programming director John Dimick's inexperience with hip-hop. Emmis Communications, the parent of Hot 97 and KISS-FM, hired Dimick in November from Jefferson-Pilot Communications in San Diego, where he oversaw country, jazz and alternative-rock stations. "It's been a zoo up there since Dimick took over. He doesn't know what he's doing," Porter says one DJ told him.

After I was quoted in the *New York Post* story, producers from Fox News' "Hannity & Colmes" did a segment with me on HOT 97's "Smackfest." That night, IndustryEars.com received more than 200,000 hits, and I started to get emails of support from all over the country.

In addition to being a fresh start, Atlanta was an education for me. I hung out at a tiny record store called Reloaded Records that sold mostly mix-tapes and DVDs like the popular SMACK DVD line. They had a large screen plasma TV on the back wall that showed the latest SMACK DVDs all day long. I knew that street DVDs existed; I'd seen them in stores, though I never paid them much attention. But I started paying attention when I hung out at Reloaded Records and saw crowds of people watching hip-hop artist Jadakiss visit a friend who was cutting up crack cocaine on camera.

I saw firsthand how different things were for the younger generation. Young guys with nicknames would wake up in the morning, smoke a blunt, go to work, come home, drink a beer, smoke another blunt, watch videos and play video games. When I was their age, I had basketball and radio. I threw parties and I worked. These young kids seemed to waste most of their time emulating hip-hop artists.

I had heard of campaigns against the record industry. C. Delores Tucker was famous — or infamous, depending on how you looked it at — for her tirades against negative lyrics. Tupac had called Tucker a "motherfucker" in one his songs. Other rappers wrote lyrics about her that made Tupac's characterization seem like a compliment. To me, hip hop was not that serious. I loved a lot of the records; even some of the gangsta rap was cool with me. I just thought they shouldn't be playing it on the airwaves for children to hear. I was not interested in carrying C. Delores Tucker's baton, but I knew something had to be done to turn this thing around.

I knew that lyrics degrading women and promoting hate and violence were having a negative influence on youth culture. I was thoroughly convinced that rap lyrics inspired Lea's father to beat her mother with a baseball bat. It was not just in my head — it was reality. Labels continued to churn out songs with violent, misogynistic lyrics, music that had no redeeming value. The great defenders of this music claimed it was the story of the streets. But there was no balance. The choice had become gangsta or nothing. Lea's generation was being exposed to music that almost exclusively had negative messages. I began to realize how blessed I was to have grown up with the music of my era.

Chapter 2: The Queens Kid

The incident with Lea made me reflect on how important music to my development. I was the only child of a single mom growing up in the Jamaica neighborhood of Queens, N.Y. and I learned a lot about life by listening to music. Popular songs highlighted topics that usually weren't discussed with children, like love and relationships. Music taught me a lot about the triumphs, struggles and challenges in life.

My mother, Lillian Porter, loved music. I remember our turntable and the 45s in different colors — yellow and brown, red and black, purple and gold. Most of my entertainment consisted of music, and the radio was always playing in the background. One of my favorite songs was Marvin Gaye and Tammi Terrell's "Ain't Nothing Like the Real Thing." It was the first record that taught me about the value of love. My parents had just divorced, and it hit home.

My mother liked to listen to Buddy Miles, The Isley Brothers, Mighty Sparrow, The Temptations, and Johnnie Taylor. I hated it when she played Taylor's "Who's Making Love" when her boyfriend Mr. Jack came around. I was about 10 years old, and I did not like the words to that song. I didn't know what making love meant, but I knew it had something to do with my mother and Mr. Jack being together. I didn't need a new daddy. I had a daddy. I was paying attention to those lyrics.

My father liked Malcolm X. Dad's real name was Xavier, but he called himself Leroy X Porter. He always wore suits; a black man had to take his dress seriously so he wouldn't be disrespected. He taught me to walk on the outside of the sidewalk and to open doors for a lady. I learned to be a gentleman by his example. My father would take me to Chinese restaurants, to the Penn Station arcade, and to James Bond movies. We went to the 1964/1965 New York World's Fair 37 times; my dad was captivated by it because he was an architect. He would take me on the Long Island Rail Road (LIRR) to travel. Though it was more expensive than the subway, the LIRR was clean and had nice seats, and the ride to Penn Station from his home in Brooklyn took just 17 minutes, compared to 45 minutes to an hour on the subway. When I was 13, I started taking the train from Queens to Brooklyn by myself to visit my dad. Coming from my all-black world, it was fascinating to visit an all-white one.

James Brown had a house on Linden Boulevard about 40 blocks from where I grew up that was surrounded by a black wrought iron fence. As kids, we used to ride bikes past the house to see if we would catch a glimpse of James Brown coming out the door. We would see his black Cadillac limousine, but we never saw him.

James Brown already had plenty of hits, but when I was 11, "Say it Loud — I'm Black and I'm Proud" came out. It was 1968, a time of real struggle. Black power and the Black power movement were in full force. I felt the power within the first few seconds of hearing the song. Black was my racial identity, after that. No longer was I Negro or Colored. No African-American for me. I was now Black with a capital B. And man, was I was proud! I recalled fights starting over someone calling someone else "Black," as if it were an insult. Those days were over! I felt the potency of that song and it shaped my thinking.

My best friends were two light-skinned, straight-haired Puerto Rican kids named Bucky and Renny. Their father, Mr. Stroud, was the first "real" music industry person I had ever met. Mr. Stroud was married to Nina Simone, and he was also her manager. I didn't know who Nina Simone was, but I knew she was a singer. In 1982, when I saw a movie that played her songs, I realized it was Mr. Stroud who ran the Black music department at RCA records. I recall one day when Cuba Gooding Sr. of The Main Ingredient walked into Mr. Stroud's office. That was a big deal for me. I said to Renny and Bucky, "Wow, your dad works with Cuba Gooding!" As Mr. Stroud's daughter said many years later, her father was the original Puff Daddy, a real black music executive.

My neighborhood was comprised mostly of single parent households, and it was the proverbial "village." All the kids played together, and any parent could tell you what to do. My mother would open the door and yell "Paul!" And all my friends would yell "Paul!"

As a kid, my favorite station was WWRL-AM Super 16 in Queens. That was the station for Black music, and Gary Byrd — who later changed his name to Imhotep Gary Byrd — was the talking DJ who recited poetry on the air. His motto was "Every brother ain't a brother. Every sister ain't a sister." He was so popular that he got a record deal. Gary Byrd and the GB Experience performed and recorded on his RCA label, Real Thing Records, and he wrote songs for other artists, including Stevie Wonder's "Village Ghetto Land" and "Black Man" featured on the classic 1976 album, *Songs in the Key of Life*. One day Gary Byrd came to our school, St. Clement Pope in South Jamaica, Queens, to talk to us about careers in the entertainment industry. I was in the seventh grade, and he made a strong impression on me.

I also met Willis Reed, a center for the New York Knicks who dated a lady who lived next door to Bucky and Renny. He inspired my love for basketball. He bought us a backboard and showed us how to shoot a jumper. Of course, he would park his car down the street so that we wouldn't hit it. In 1970, the Knicks won the championship with Reed, one of our mentors, on this team. In 1996, he was voted one of the 50 Greatest Players in NBA History.

As kids, we played basketball, stickball, and kickball against other blocks. That's how I met my friend Lynn Staton, whose father was also in the music business and lived one street over. I played basketball with Lynn's brother. One day, Lynn asked me to play doctor, and we've been friends ever since.

I attended Christ the King Regional High School. I went from attending a 98 percent black school at St. Clement Pope that was two blocks from my home to attending a 98 percent white high school that was a two-hour bus ride from my home. It was a culture shock traveling to the white part of Queens. I made the basketball team and tried to stay alive. My friend Bucky came to Christ the King the next year; and when I was in 10th grade, his brother Renny joined us.

In high school, I spent a lot of my time focusing on basketball and helped Christ the King make it to New York City's Final Four. I didn't have time for much else, but by now I had a radio in my room and my interest in music was growing.

There were three radio stations that black people listened to during that time: WWRL-AM, where Gary Byrd was king; WABC-AM, which played crossover Black music, including the sounds of Motown; and most importantly, WBLS-FM, a black-owned station that was home to the great Frankie Crocker. You knew it was 8 p.m., when you heard Frankie sign off with his signature song "Moody's Mood for Love" by King Pleasure. Then Frankie would announce: "If Frankie Crocker is not on your radio, your radio is not on." Anyone who was black and lived within the range of WBLS knew his voice.

In 1974, when I was 15 years old, my father bought me my first album, the Ohio Players' "Honey." That was a big deal for me, as I don't recall my father ever listening to music. Later that same year, I went with Bucky and Renny to see the Ohio Players perform at Radio City Music Hall. We took the subway into the city with no adult supervision. I had music on my mind.

I graduated from high school in 1975 and planned to attend St. Mary's College in Kansas on a basketball scholarship. I'd visited St. Mary's and was all set to go. Then, I fell in love with a girl named JoAnn whom I'd met through our mutual friend Lynn. JoAnn got sick and was hospitalized. Lynn asked me to visit her in the hospital, and I did. JoAnn told me she was sick because of a Vitamin D deficiency. By the time she was back at home, I was in love with her. After basketball practice, I'd take the bus to her house, stop for a quart of milk and bring it to her.

After a few months of innocent dates over glasses of milk, JoAnn's mother had had enough.

"JoAnn! Tell this boy what's really wrong with you!" she yelled. JoAnn refused to say a word.

"Paul, honey," JoAnn's mother said to me. "JoAnn has sickle cell anemia."

I thought that was just a fancy word for a Vitamin D deficiency. "I know," I said, holding up the carton. "That's why we're drinking milk!"

JoAnn was my very first girlfriend. Suddenly, Kansas seemed too far away to go to school. My mother was crushed that I'd turned down the opportunity to go to St. Mary's. It was too late to go anywhere else, so I enrolled at LaGuardia Community College. JoAnn and Lynn went off together to Northeastern University in Boston. I didn't know anything about Boston or Northeastern except that my girlfriend was there. I asked my high school basketball coach to help me get into Northeastern, and he did. My mother was disappointed that I was not going to Kansas. All I knew was that I had to be in Boston with JoAnn.

Chapter 3: Music Education

I convinced my mother to let me stay in Boston the summer before my sophomore year began. Lynn's father, Mr. Staton — who was a promoter at Atlantic Records — sent me off with a box of records to sell. It was an omen. I ended up giving the records to a popular record store called Skippy White's, located on Columbus Avenue. My education in the world of music and radio was about to begin.

Of course, JoAnn and I were inseparable. I kept a copy of her schedule taped to my notebook, and she taped mine to hers. I started out as an accounting major. I hated school but I loved basketball, which turned out to be my bridge to music. I couldn't play basketball during my first quarter because the season had already started, but I practiced with the team and hung out with my friend Smiley, who I knew from playing basketball in Queens. During the next summer, my coach asked if I'd be willing to stay in Boston to continue practicing with the team in preparation for the next season.

I said yes, which set me on a path that would affect the rest of my life. If I wasn't practicing basketball, there wasn't much to do in Boston. This was 1977, and there were riots breaking out in South Boston over black students being bused to schools in white neighborhoods. It wasn't safe for black students to socialize off campus, so I stayed in the gym. Eventually, Smiley invited me to hang out with him at the college radio station, WRBB.

We entered a small, dark room with a control board and a set of turntables in front and another set of turntables to the far right. There were black light posters on the walls and people smoking weed; the students were mature and refined — everything I wasn't. I was a tall, skinny virgin who had never smoked or drank. Just watching the seniors running the radio station late at night intoxicated me.

I spent all my free time that summer at WRBB. I started out just answering the request lines. Eventually, I started sitting in for entire shows, learning how to run the boards, push the buttons, put in the cart machines that held the music, adjust the volume and the levels, play the voice-overs that identified the station and hit the turntables to start the music — all of the technical aspects of broadcasting.

Northeastern is a nearly all-white school in a nearly all-white city, but it's located right next to Roxbury, the black section of Boston. I quickly learned that the black community at Northeastern was like a close-knit family, meeting up at the quad to shoot the breeze and just hang out. It was an unwritten rule that if you were a black student at Northeastern, you listened to WRBB at midnight, when a show called "Soul's Place" was on the air. During the day, WRBB was all white, but they let the black folks on the air at night.

As I learned more and more about radio, my interest in music grew. I decided to invest in a mixer so that I could learn how to be a DJ. Smiley played the music at a lot of the college parties, but he couldn't blend records — they collided. We called Smiley "The Train Wreck." He would bring in a new song, and it would be off beat and everyone would stop dancing.

I studied beats per minute so that when I blended and overlaid records people would say, *Awe, yeah! That's my song!* I grew up quite a bit in the summer of '77. I was on my own in a brand-new city, and I'd discovered a new love to add to JoAnn and basketball — radio. After a few days at the station, I said to myself, *you can do this; you can do radio.* I was gifted with the stereotypical voice of a radio jock, but I had never paid attention to it before. I had been too busy playing basketball. I replaced my love for the crossover dribble with a deep and abiding love for music.

When the fall quarter began, they gave me a radio show on WRBB. My shift was Sunday night from midnight to 3 a.m. Everyone at the station had a theme song, and I'd decided mine would be "Pure Love," named after an instrumental by John Klemmer. On the night of my first show, it was the first song I played as I introduced myself. I signed on using a bass-deep, sexy voice, *"This is Paul Pure Love Porter,"* and you couldn't tell me I wasn't the man. I even made my own promotions. I ripped off a James Brown live performance: His hype-man introduced him and said something like: *"Ladies and gentlemen, there are seven wonders of the world. You're about to hear the eighth. It's star time! This man is mean..."*

Now, I had JoAnn, basketball, and radio. School came fourth, and my grades reflected that, as I struggled to juggle a full load of classes. Part of the problem was my shift — midnight to 3 a.m. — was not a convenient time slot. When I should have been sleeping or studying, I was at the station. I was hooked on radio, and I wasn't about to give up my slot. I just needed a better one.

At that time, the black students at Northeastern were lucky they had slots at all. I thought there was no way those in control would allow black students to have funk and soul playing during the day. The school was predominately white, and whites were running the place, including the radio station, which had a white Program Director and a white Music Director. I was determined to get a better shift, so I started paying attention to the business side of the station to see how I could make it happen. I realized that it was a numbers game; people ran for positions and the majority ruled. It was that simple. After basketball season ended in January, I decided I would run for General Manager. While most people at the station were probably majoring in communications and planning to work in radio after college, I didn't know what I was going to do. I just wanted to be General Manager so I could give myself a better shift.

Anyone at the school could be a member of the station. All they had to do was attend three consecutive Monday night meetings. There were 36 white members and 12 black members. I started forcing all my friends — even the ones who had no interest in radio — to come out to the meetings. Every week, there were more and more Afros sitting up in the station. No one seemed to notice my plan. When I ran for General Manager, I won easily, thanks to all my friends who became members just in time for the elections.

Every DJ who had a show had to reapply for their time slot. I looked over all the applications, put together the new schedule and those cats had a *fit*. Of course, I put myself on during the best time slot. Now, almost all of the black DJs had shows on during the day. No more relegating Black music to nighttime — I had the funk playing 24 hours a day. I assigned the white DJs Saturday nights and they went to the administration to complain, but their complaints went ignored. I'd followed the rules; I was voted in as General Manager fair and square, and I could program the station however I wanted to. This was one of my first experiences with taking on the system, and it felt good. I had the slot I wanted, and I completely overhauled the radio station.

Radio was overtaking my love for basketball. I wasn't getting a lot of playing time on the court. Then, I got suspended for leaving town during the season without telling my coach, even though I felt had a good excuse: I was walking across campus one afternoon when I saw JoAnn on her way to class, but she was coming from the wrong direction. I learned that she was messing around with someone else behind my back. JoAnn and I argued right there outside. I was devastated. She was my first — in everything. I've always been sensitive and emotional. When I realized that JoAnn had cheated on me, I left campus and caught a bus back home to New York, just like that.

I came back to school to find out that I had been suspended from the basketball team for going AWOL. My grades were suffering because I was all over the place. I ended up dropping three classes and spending even more time at the radio station. WRBB probably saved me from falling apart after JoAnn broke my heart.

We jammed at WRBB. We had no commercials, just an occasional public service announcement. The station started to get a great reputation in the Boston area, and we were able to get real acts to come in for interviews and performances, including Roy

Ayers, Parliament, The Ohio Players, and New Birth. I became the Program Director at WRBB. We changed to a 24-hour black station, and from 1976 to 1996, WRBB stayed black at the predominately white university.

WRBB started showing up in the ratings, even though it wasn't a commercial radio station and only had a 10-watt signal that extended just 15 miles from campus. Arbitron, the company that collects data on radio stations, gives out journals to a cross-section of people in a particular market to figure out which stations they're listening to. It turned out that listeners were starting to write in WRBB in their journals, and the station began showing up in the ratings! I knew things had changed when I started getting packages full of albums from local record reps. The labels wanted to make sure we had the hot new records.

I was deeply rooted in music and radio. It wasn't long before I teamed up with Harold Austin, a Northeastern student who had a show on WRBB, to start a party business called HAPPY: Harold Austin, Paul Porter and You. We would make $250 per party, which was big money for college students. Once, we held a party at Boston University's George Sherman Union with more than 900 people in attendance. We started clearing $1000 per party,

Mercyline "Mike" Bernardo, who was the Northeast rep at Columbia Records, saw what was going on at WRBB and sent us two boxes of records with 100 albums each from artists such as Earth, Wind & Fire, Heatwave, and The Isley Brothers. I went to New York to meet Mike. She took me to lunch and let me have carte blanche at Columbia. This was the beginning of WRBB's rise to the top. We gave away tickets to shows. We were making connections with major record labels and artists. We knew the people in the bands — the drummer for The Ohio Players and Patryce "Chocolate" Banks from Grand Central Station, to name a few. I remember New Birth and Jeffrey Osborne of LTD coming up to visit WRBB. Earl Sellers, a record representative from MCA Records, sent me 50 copies of *Galaxy* by War, and I was thrilled. I gave a copy to everyone at the station and still had 30 to use for on-air contests. Mike Bernardo sent new music too.

By 1978, WRBB was so popular in Boston that I received a call from Sunny Joe White, Program Director at WILD, the Black AM daytime station in Boston. We'd started showing up in the Nielsen ratings, and we were taking listeners away from his station. He said he'd heard good things about WRBB and wanted to let me know he was listening.

Sunny Joe said he'd like me to come in and intern at WILD, but I didn't get back to him right away. For one thing, WILD was an AM station, and to me that just wasn't cool. Plus, even though WILD was an all-black station, the jocks all talked in the high-pitched, white boy rapid-fire voice that they used on mainstream radio. Furthermore, I was already *the man* at WRBB. I was running the station, and I had my own show. By this time, my boy Harold Austin and I were noted for throwing our HAPPY parties in Boston.

Sunny would call me up occasionally to chat, and once, he called with a gift — tickets to see James Brown. A free live show was more than I could fathom. I wondered how Sunny Joe could part with something so valuable. I decided there might be something to learn from commercial radio. Soon after the show, I met with him at WILD's office. Sunny Joe was a little guy, about 5'8", and I knew right away that he was openly homosexual, which was an oddity in the '70s, at least for me. He was flamboyant, bubbly, and animated — a black man with pressed red hair and a high-energy AM radio voice.

Sunny became my first boss in radio and my mentor. "K.I.S.S.," he would say. "'Keep it Simple, Stupid,' so everyone can understand." WILD was a sunrise to sunset station and still operates that way today. Sunny was way ahead of his time. His philosophy was more music, less talk. He made you condense your speech and would call you on the hotline if you talked too much. He wanted the music to be the star.

At first, I would go in only on music day, when Sunny Joe would meet with various record reps and listen to their new releases to decide what he would add to the station's playlist. The reps from New York would usually drive up together, stopping at music meetings in Hartford along the way. It was my job to seat the reps in the lobby and bring them in, one by one, to meet with Sunny Joe. I'd take their vinyl records to the turntable in Sunny Joe's office and play the music. I'd give my opinion if Sunny Joe asked me, and then we'd all talk about the artist and maybe listen to some other tracks on the album. Then Sunny would have me leave and go get the next rep.

It was in the lobby of WILD that I first met some of the people I would work with in future years. I met Ruben Rodriguez, a friendly guy who worked for Casablanca Records. And I met Sylvia Rhone, then a record rep. Sylvia was the finest woman I'd ever seen in my life. She had soft features, an amazing body, and a bright smile. I remember shaking her hand the first day I met her. She was only about five years older than me, but I was in college, so it felt like she was light years ahead of me. She asked me questions about the classes I was taking and where I was from, and I was awestruck. A grown woman who worked in the record industry and looked like a supermodel was actually talking to me? I really looked forward to seeing her at the music meetings.

"What do you like to eat, Paul?" she asked me after one meeting.

I shrugged my shoulders and said something stupid about eating pizza. Sylvia laughed. "Next week, I'm taking you out to lunch. We're going to Aku Aku," she said.

It was a fancy Chinese restaurant in the lobby of WILD's office building. Chinese food alone was still exotic to me, so I was bowled over when Sylvia took me out the next week to a real restaurant with tablecloths and waiters. She paid the bill without a second thought. I couldn't imagine what she could possibly see in me. It never occurred to me that what she saw was my proximity to Sunny Joe's ear. I actually thought she had a crush on me.

Eventually, WILD took over my life, and I dropped out of college during my senior year. Sunny Joe gave me the opportunity to go on the air. He hired me as a part-time jock for $10,000 per year. I left my "Pure Love" moniker and my naturally deep voice at WRBB. This was a Black daytime station, so I had to learn how to use my upper register. I started work at 5 a.m. as a fill-in for a gospel show. I was happy to have the job. I'd announce cheerfully, "1090 WILD Boston. This is Paul Porter."

Sunny Joe still had me sit in on the music meetings. He knew I was a big part of the reason why WRBB developed a great reputation, and he trusted my ear. Actually, Sunny Joe didn't have much of an ear for music. He just knew how to surround himself with people who did.

During one meeting, Sharon Heyward asked about one of her artists, Evelyn "Champagne" King. Sharon had brought the song "Shame" in to Sunny Joe, but months later, he still wasn't playing the record. Sharon asked me what I thought of the record, and Sunny Joe looked carefully at me for my response. I told Sharon the truth. I'd played the hell out of the record at WRBB, and everybody hit the dance floor when I played it at college parties. Sharon gave Sunny Joe a look. The song went into rotation that same week on WILD and it took off in Boston, then nationwide, eventually selling half a million copies.

I was fascinated that one radio station could have such an impact. The song had already been popular in clubs for close to a year, so I didn't "break" the record. But as soon as I nudged Sunny Joe into playing it, other Program Directors around the country followed suit, and the song really took off. I began to trust my ear more and more. In my record pool, I heard local Boston crooner Maurice Starr's 12-inch and recommended him to Sharon. He was eventually signed to RCA. Although his solo career was short-lived, he used the money he'd earned to return to Roxbury and start the group New Edition, who would also be signed to RCA.

The following year, a new FM station that was starting in Boston, Kiss 108, recruited Sunny Joe to be the Program Director. I actually cried when he left. He said in his farewell meeting that because of contractual issues with WILD, he couldn't take any of us with him to the new station.

I'd learned so much from Sunny Joe about the commercial world of music that I decided I would continue to learn from him. Although I never worked for him again, for the rest of my career, I never made a major career decision without checking in with Sunny Joe. I've worked with some major names in radio and video over the years, and Sunny Joe is up there with the best of them. I always felt like he was protecting me from the seedier side of radio.

Sunny Joe went to great extremes to keep me shielded from anything scandalous. All I knew about payola in those days were the old Alan Freed stories from the '50s. And I saw the looks that radio executives exchanged when certain names came up, like Frankie Crocker. Sunny Joe's commitment to keeping up a professional appearance just made it that much more difficult for me to adjust to his replacement.

Chapter 4: Music as Business

Sunny Joe left WILD to work at Kiss 108 in 1979. WILD hired Steve Crumbley, "The Seventh Son," as the new Program Director. Steve was crude, crass, and loud. I disliked him immediately. He was the first person who made me keenly aware of payola.

In the music industry, payola is the illegal practice of record companies secretly providing incentives and special favors or paying outright bribes to disc jockeys in exchange for radio play. Record reps wine and dine DJs, send them cash, buy them cars and set up trips to get their songs on the air. Under U.S. law, radio stations *can* play specific songs in exchange for money, but this has to be disclosed on the air as sponsored time and cannot be counted as regular airplay.

"Man, you gotta learn how to *work* radio," Steve said. I had no idea what he was talking about. "You see my car?" he asked. Steve had a black Buick Regal with red leather seats and shiny rims. "Mille Jackson bought me that car 'cause I played her songs," he bragged. It was the first time I'd heard someone openly admitting to playing records for compensation. I was disgusted.

Steve was a showman who believed in building his brand as an individual. He wanted super personalities who talked a lot. His philosophy was the opposite of Sunny Joe's, who liked to keep the talk short and sweet. Steve used me to learn about the city of Boston, but he never helped me become a better jock. I thought he was going to fire me because I was Sunny Joe's protégé, but he said, "Hey man, I'm gon' give you a shot 'cause you sound pretty good." Actually, he kept me around for another reason: I knew music and I was popular in Boston. For the next three months, I had to take Steve Crumbley to the clubs I was spinning at so he could get a feel for Boston and the music scene. I sat in on all of his music meetings, just as I'd done with Sunny Joe. Steve was constantly pumping me for information and advice.

Then, he fired one of the jocks, and I got nervous. Steve had assured me my job was safe, but I was not naïve enough to believe him. The following Saturday, I came in for my shift. While I was on the air, I looked through the window and saw Steve walking by. He never came in to work on the weekend. I was suspicious. As soon as I got off the air, he told me he wanted to talk to me. He said something about me needing more experience; that I should try to find work in a smaller market. He told me he was going to have to let me go. He also said something about hoping that I would understand. I was furious. I felt used and abused.

I met my replacement that same day. He was already hanging out at the office. His name was "Butterball" and he was a carbon copy of Steve Crumbley, with a jheri curl, gold teeth, and long polished nails. I could not believe it! One of my friends who worked at WILD after I left told me Steve Crumbley eventually replaced just about every jock with his jheri curl-wearing, gold tooth-sporting clones.

I was still throwing parties all over Boston, and I was still affiliated with WRBB, although I was no longer a student at Northeastern. Getting fired from WILD hurt my feelings. I didn't like what Steve Crumbley represented: the slick talk, the scandalous behavior, and the payola. He didn't care about the music. He only cared about the money. I did not respect him.

Just a few years in radio had opened my eyes. I experienced payola — not up close, but I knew it was there. I saw the influence radio could have on the music industry, and after Steve fired me, I learned industry rule number 4,080: *Record company people are shady.*

Not one of the record reps I'd befriended reached out to me or returned my calls. I went back to the WILD building the week after I was fired. I stood outside, waiting for the record reps to come in for the music meeting. The only thing I heard was "sorry to hear that" and "talk to you later." I took their lack of support personally, because I didn't know better.

Not long after, I got a job as Program Director at an AM radio station in Cambridge: WCAS. It was another station that shut down at sunset, and it was a piece of crap. They had a low, 250-watt signal; it was a bootleg operation. Worst of all, it was like a crapshoot to get paid. The station struggled to make ends meet, so when payday came around, I had to haul my behind to the bank on my lunch break to get my check cashed. There were far too many times when I would come running into the bank later in the day only for the manager to stop me to say they weren't cashing any WCAS checks.

I sold records from my collection to the local record shop to supplement my income. I was not happy. Steve Crumbley had taken over Sunny Joe's station and replaced me with a Butterball. No one in Boston could hear me on the air at WCAS. I was ready to go.

In radio, once you get that first gig, it's easy to keep a job — that is, if you're willing to relocate to Podunk cities across the country. I was not. I liked big cities like Boston and New York, and I wanted to live near my friends and family. I had to be in the best markets, right away. I was a cocky kid, and I didn't think it should be any other way.

After a trip to Washington, D.C. to hang out with a friend who went to Howard University, I knew my days in Boston were numbered. We visited NBC's studios in 1980. As we pulled into NBC's parking lot, all I saw were luxury vehicles. I met Willard Scott, Bryant Gumbel, and Katie Couric.

Then, the radio station, WKYS, caught my eye. As soon as I saw it, I knew I wanted to work there. At WKYS they had engineers, so the DJs never had to touch a record, unlike my gig in Boston, where I was the DJ, the engineer, and the janitor. WKYS was a first-class operation, and I wanted to be a part of it. As soon as I got back to Boston, I put together a tape and started sending it out. I got a copy of *Black Radio Exclusive* and looked up WKYS to find out the name of the Program Director: Donnie Simpson.

A few weeks later, I came home from my radio gig at WCAS and my then-girlfriend told me I'd gotten a letter from NBC. I was so excited to see the NBC logo on the envelope, but I opened it only to find a rejection letter from Donnie. He said he wasn't looking for anyone and that I needed a little work. He advised me to start using my diaphragm. At that point, I had been working in radio for over five years, but I knew nothing about using my diaphragm to better my voice. I took Donnie's advice, and a few months later I sent him another tape. This time, I heard back from his secretary — NBC wanted to talk to me.

NBC flew me down to D.C. first class on a snowy night in December of 1981 and put me up in the Hyatt in Georgetown. As I got out of the cab, I saw Donnie Simpson's brown Monte Carlo with WKYS license plates pulling up to the hotel. I checked into my room and Donnie called, telling me to meet him and his wife at the hotel restaurant. I put on one of the only two suits I owned and went up to the restaurant for a meeting that would change the course of my life.

The Simpsons were warm and friendly. I remember thinking that I wasn't just being offered a job; I was being introduced to a new way of life. They were smooth, refined, and classy. They smelled like money, and it was clear that WKYS had been good to them. It was the most expensive meal I'd ever had in my entire life.

I was hoping Donnie would hire me as a part-time employee. I was eager to accept a position. One day's pay at WKYS would be more than one week's pay at my gig in Boston. Plus, the station was located in Washington, D.C., a.k.a. "Chocolate City." Most importantly, WKYS was *the* station. Their main competition was Howard University's WHUR-FM, which was owned by the school but managed by professionals. Donnie explained to me that there was only one other black jock, Candy Shannon, at WKYS and that he wanted me to come on board.

"So," I said to Donnie, "What day do I have?" I assumed he would try me out on a temporary basis to fill in for some shifts and maybe give me one weekly shift of my own.

Donnie's green eyes twinkled and he smiled. "This is full-time," he said. "I'm starting a brand new shift for you. The show is called Night Flight 93. It's from 10 p.m. to 2 a.m. How's that sound?"

How did it sound? It sounded as sweet as my favorite slow jam. He pulled out a 33-page, three-year contract to review. I immediately flipped to the page with my salary details. My starting salary was $33,500 with six weeks of vacation each year. In 1982, that was real good money. After two years, my salary would nearly double to $66,000. I thought I'd won the lottery.

"Can you start on the fourth?" he asked.

"I'm there," I told him.

"Oh, and you have a new name," Donnie said, leaning back in his chair. "You're Paul 'The Captain' Porter."

The Captain? I thought it was the corniest name I'd ever heard. I protested, telling Donnie that I'd rather just be Paul Porter.

"Well," he said, "on that one, you don't have a choice." Donnie motioned for the check and then flashed me his megawatt smile.

Everything else about the gig was turning out to be perfect. I'd be doing what I loved, and the money would be more than I'd ever made. Donnie told me that I'd be involved with the programming department as well. He expected me to come to the music meetings and help decide what would be played on the air. I felt like Donnie had a plan for me. I felt that he was going to be a friend, not just my boss. He told me later that he already knew about me, even before I sent him a tape. It turns out his twin sister lived in Roxbury. She'd listened to my show on WRBB and told Donnie about how good she thought I was. Donnie said that when he came up to Boston to visit his sister, he made a point to tune in to my show. Everything seemed to be coming together the way it was meant to, except that I was about to be stuck with a corny name.

Promotions announcing my show were on the air before I arrived, and Donnie had everything set up when I started my shift on January 4, 1982. As I sat down to play my first record, I wondered if I could really play whatever I wanted. I was about to find out.

The first song I played on WKYS was Sly and the Family Stone's "Sex Machine," a song from the 1969 album *Stand*. The song was 13 minutes and 45 seconds of mostly instrumental music. After a crazy drum solo at the end, they sang: *"We blew your mind out."* The phone line started blowing up. When I got to my first commercial break, Donnie called in and said: "You're going to be a big star in this town. I'm glad to have you."

"As long as I'm here," he said, "you'll always have a job. Now get back to work." Donny was happy, and I was happy.

It was a community-oriented station. We hosted pool parties and softball and basketball games. We were out in the streets meeting people. The WKYS van roamed around town giving out prizes. Our events drew thousands of people — even stars like boxing great Sugar Ray Leonard.

Donnie was a great leader. He put together a strong team, and he trusted his people to do their jobs. Candy Shannon and Jeff Leonard, both great jocks, were on board. It was a union shop, so everything was state of the art and we were making good money. I went from making zero dollars at 500-watt WILD in Boston that went off the air at 4:55 p.m. to making top dollar at 50,000-watt WKYS in Washington, D.C. I had arrived!

Donnie's music philosophy was like playing the hits in your parent's basement. The top songs were played every three to four hours, not every hour like they do today. Before corporations took over radio playlists, Program Directors like Donnie Simpson used their ears to determine which songs would be played, and from day one he let me control a huge part of the rotation at WKYS.

I exposed D.C. listeners to a lot of music. I'd play older songs I liked and then get requests for them like they were brand new records. I played the classic club joint "Must Be the Music" by Secret Weapon, and it exploded like it was a new single, even though it had been released when I was back in Boston. One night, I played a set of songs by Brenda Russell, who'd had some success with "If Only for One Night," a song that Luther Vandross would later make famous.

"It sure would be good to hear something new from Brenda Russell," I said. I heard from a few callers who agreed with me. And then, a few days later, I heard from Brenda. A friend in D.C. heard my show and told Brenda that a D.C. jock was yearning to hear new music from her, and she wanted to thank me. It was something simple — I was just playing her music and thinking out loud. But it meant something to her. Brenda went back to writing and recording and soon hit it big with her album *Get Here*, featuring the hit record "Piano in The Dark." That's why I loved being in radio. I can't sing a note, and I never played an instrument. But I enjoy music, and I was able to bring it to the masses in my own way.

During my second week in town, Donnie Simpson threw a party for me in Silver Springs, Md., at his well-appointed ranch house with a huge basement lined with gold records from dozens of artists. Most of the staffers from WKYS were there, black and white people, which was new for me. At most stations, things were so segregated that no one hung out together. But at my welcome-to-WKYS soiree, I partied hard with folks of all hues.

I was a long way from my last gig at WCAS, where the radio signal was weak, the paychecks often bounced, and I had a pathetic midday slot. Donnie took a personal interest in me, and I believed he wanted me to succeed. But he wasn't taking me under his wing just because he liked me. I was part of Donnie's plan to shake things up at WKYS. The station was already beating out its closest competitors in urban music, and Donnie wanted to be Number 1 overall in the marketplace.

Donnie trusted my ear for music. I think he valued that more than my talent as a jock. He knew that in Boston, I programmed my show and decided what was played, and the people were feeling it. In D.C., Donnie depended on Joe Alfenito to pick the records, but Joe did not have a good ear for music. He gave Donnie whatever the reps from the record labels recommended to him. Donnie knew he couldn't put me on as Music Director, so he did the next best thing. He brought me in to be his second set of ears.

I played whatever I wanted, regardless of what was on the playlist, because Donnie trusted me. If it was raining, I might play "Cloudy" by Average White Band. When I was in love (which was all the time) I'd play "Chocolate Girl" by The Whispers. If I found an obscure song that l liked, I'd play it as often as I wanted. Eventually, my listeners would request the song.

That's exactly what happened with a little-known track from the group Luther, featuring Luther Vandross and four other members. When I was still in Boston, I'd picked up their self-titled album at a record store. That was around 1981, when Luther Vandross' debut solo album, *Never Too Much*, came out on Epic Records; it was a smash success, and every station was playing the hell out of tracks like "A House Is Not A Home," "She's a Super Lady" and the title track. Even though Luther Vandross refused to do radio interviews, he was *the man*, and he was in heavy rotation everywhere.

I loved *Never Too Much* as much as everyone else. But I couldn't stop playing this one song I'd heard on the old *Luther* album. It was called "The Second Time Around." I've always been a sucker for a great ballad, and this was one of the best. I played it in Boston and took it with me to D.C. to add to my personal playlist there.

This was a time when radio DJs would bring their own records to a new job. Today, a jock from a small town can show up for his first day at a station in Los Angeles and be prepared for work. He doesn't need to know what the audience likes and he doesn't need to bring his own flavor to the station. All of the decisions have already been made. All he needs to do is talk. But back then, DJs had more control over the programming, so I started playing "The Second Time Around" on WKYS, and listeners began to request it. After a while, Luther Vandross' record label, Epic, began getting record requests from retailers in the D.C. area, because customers were coming in and asking to buy a copy of the album. The only problem was, the song wasn't *on* Epic Records. The group had recorded it for Cotillion Records, a small boutique label. And of course, the folks at Epic didn't want anyone trying to find that record instead of *Never Too Much*, which had already sold a half million copies.

Donnie Simpson got a call from Lynda Penn, the head of radio promotions at Epic. She asked Donnie who was playing that record and *why*. Donnie explained to her that I loved the song and my listeners were requesting it. He wasn't going to tell me to stop playing it. I was doing exactly what he brought me down there to do — shake things up and play music the listeners enjoyed. The retailers were driving Lynda crazy, and she had to find a solution. Luther Vandross ended up re-recording the song and Epic released it on his next album.

When he came to town later that year for a show at the Capital Centre, he made sure I was invited and arranged to meet me after the show. According to the folks at Epic, he wanted to meet the man who had the audacity to force him to re-record his own song. I met him backstage and he shook my hand firmly and said, simply, "Thank you."

Donnie's management style of trusting me to do my job without interfering worked well. When I arrived at WKYS, WHUR was Number 1, WOOK was Number 2, and WOL was Number 3. Donnie Simpson's show was Number 1, but WKYS was not. Three months after I arrived, which is how often the stations were ranked, WKYS was Number 1 overall.

I moved into an apartment near the radio station, got a new girlfriend and settled into life in D.C. Donnie and I hung out all the time. We played together on the WKYS basketball team. If Donnie had an extra ticket to an event, I would go with him. My new girlfriend was Donnie's wife's best friend, which brought us all even closer together.

I watched Donnie and learned. At dinner with Donnie, I saw the corporate side of radio — fancy restaurants, contracts and plans for the future. Then I met Isaac, a shady record promotion man for a major record label, and learned how almost everyone else played the game. Isaac put me on to easy women, a quick high and plans for the night. Isaac and Donnie were on opposite ends of the spectrum when it came to power and corruption. To this day, Donnie Simpson is the purest, cleanest guy I've known in radio. You won't find anyone who can tell you he's ever been caught up in corruption of any kind.

I'd heard my share of scandalous stories about payola, but you couldn't tell me that accepting favors from Isaac was illegal. As far as I was concerned, he was a nice guy with an expense account who hooked me up with women, fine dinners and whatever else I wanted. Who could say no to that? I rationalized that this was the same as getting basketball tickets and good seats at concerts. But it wasn't the same. This was payola, and it had taken only a few months for me to get mixed up in it. My association with someone as clean and corporate as Donnie Simpson didn't shield me from the lure of corruption. Isaac was a man with a plan. It was his job to make sure I was happy. Initially, Isaac didn't ask me for favors. He just showed me a good time and introduced me to everyone I needed to know.

I fit into D.C. easily — a little too easily. Time seemed to fly by. Later that year, I was invited to a party to celebrate a new Diana Ross single. The song, "Muscles," wasn't a great track. The party, however, more than made up for it. It was held at the Vista International Hotel in Northwest D.C., the same hotel Marion Barry would get busted in a few years later. As soon as I stepped into the party, there were strict instructions. Instead of a coat check, they had a *clothing* check. Everyone had to strip down to their underwear and put on togas. The rooms were decked out with bars, cocaine was piled up on trays, and Jacuzzis and hot tubs were filled with people getting it on.

I stumbled out of that hotel at 8 o'clock the next morning. Still high, I made my way to 16th Street, where I'd parked my BMW. That toga party would never be topped — ever. I'd never seen anything wilder before that and I haven't since.

I was realizing that something Bill Staton — my friend Lynn's father — had told me was true. Mr. Staton was the former head of promotion at Atlantic Records, and when he heard I was getting into radio, he warned me about the music industry crowd, saying they were all into drugs. He was right. The record industry was all about excess and decadence. By the time I realized it, I was in way over my head.

I was doing drugs and I was partying hard, but I still took my job seriously. Ultimately, for me it was all about the music. I wouldn't play just anything. For example, Amii Stewart, who had a hit with the song "Knock on Wood" in 1979, couldn't get any airplay for her next album. Even though her label, Ariola Records, offered incentives to anyone who would play her new record, we weren't biting at WKYS. Her record was no good, plain and simple. I would not play songs I didn't like.

I was beginning to understand why people like Isaac were being nice to me. Isaac began to ask me to add certain records to my playlist. I declined and told him he had to talk to Joe about that. I did go into the office twice a week to assist Joe with arranging the playlists, and I did sit in all of the music meetings and offer my opinion when I was asked, but I wasn't crossing the line to tell Donnie to play *anything.* If Isaac was disappointed that I wasn't making it happen, he didn't show it. He still made sure I was always happy, supplying me with whatever I requested.

By this point, there was small-time corruption everywhere. There were always little incentives here and there — concert tickets, free music and flights to Los Angeles on a whim. But corruption had yet to fully explode. Before payola would heavily impact the music industry, something else would dramatically change it: the music video.

I grew up seeing bands perform live. I saw greats like James Brown, and Prince during the *Purple Rain* days, when he sold out seven straight nights at the Capital Centre. At that time, seeing a live performance was the closest you could get to your favorite artists. So when I saw the first music videos, I wasn't impressed. Watching someone act — usually poorly — while lip syncing wasn't exactly thrilling.

I saw many of these poorly made early music videos when I got a TV show my second year at WKYS. Kathy McCampbell, the Program Director for WRC TV, an NBC-owned station, asked if I'd be interested in hosting an in-house show that NBC was producing, and I said yes. It was a Saturday morning show where I would play videos, interview celebrities, and discuss topics that young adults were interested in. Kathy told me to come up with a name for the show. I called it "Fresh" after a song by Kool & The Gang.

It was tough for me to get the hang of television. I really had no business being there. I read each word off the teleprompter individually, not as part of a sentence. I couldn't keep track of what camera I was supposed to look at or how I was supposed to tilt my head. It would take me multiple takes to get through a 30-second promotion. I was a mess. So I signed myself up for private broadcasting lessons. I learned how to rewrite copy to make it sound authentic. I listened closely to Kathy and the producers on set, who also worked with experienced TV personalities like Bryant Gumbel. After a few months, I got the hang of it.

I enjoyed seeing myself on television, and the pay wasn't bad either. On top of my rapidly increasing salary at WKYS, I was making a few hundred dollars per show for "Fresh," and I received half my rate when the show repeated on Sunday mornings. "Fresh" wasn't particularly groundbreaking, but we had our high moments. My first interviewee was Jesse Johnson from The Time. Later, I interviewed singers like Stacy Lattisaw and Johnny Gill, local athletes and local politicians like then-Mayor Marion Barry. I had James Mtume on the show when Mtume's hit record "Juicy Fruit" was on the air. With risqué lyrics like *"I'll be your lollipop/You can lick me everywhere,"* "Juicy Fruit" was considered scandalous at the time, but Mtume had a different agenda on the show. He was politically astute and discussed issues like black musicians getting nose jobs and white groups like Hall and Oates threatening the future of soul music. When it came to music, Mtume was creative and bold, and when it came to politics, he was not afraid to discuss issues that were important to the black community. I can't say the same for some of the "artists" who are producing salacious music today.

Everyone had side jobs at WKYS. I worked at "Fresh," Joe Alfenito programmed a video show called "Music Video Connection" and Donnie hosted a show called "Video Soul" on a new network called BET. In the early days, BET's owner, Bob Johnson, rented a studio in Arlington, Va., for two hours a day. I visited the studio with Donnie one day and watched him do his show. I wasn't impressed at all. The channel didn't have its own studio, and the one they were using was rinky-dink and cheap, especially when compared to NBC's setup. It's hard to imagine now, but "Fresh," my local show, was bigger than anything happening on BET.

In D.C., most black folks didn't have cable in the early '80s, and for those who did, most cable companies weren't yet offering BET. I turned up my nose at Bob Johnson's BET, just like I turned up my nose at Cathy Hughes' AM station WOL when Isaac took me there to visit. They were black-owned businesses, but they didn't seem to be going anywhere. Little did I know that, years later, I would end up playing an integral role in both companies.

After two years, "Fresh" ended, and Joe Alfenito brought me over to "Music Video Connection." I started out co-hosting with my WKYS colleague Candy Shannon. Eventually, I did the show by myself, taping from popular nightclubs like The Classics in Maryland and Hogate's on D.C.'s Southwest waterfront.

"Music Video Connection" quickly became the Number 1 show on Friday nights in D.C. It came on right after the local news, and it was the place where everyone could tune in and see their favorite artists. It was then that I started to realize how powerful music videos could be.

I interviewed a host of artists for "Music Video Connection," from En Vogue and Bell Biv DeVoe to MC Hammer. These artists were selling millions of records, so what were they doing on a local television show? It was simple. In the days before MTV and BET took over music, record labels would take exposure anywhere they could get it. Being on the Number 1 show in D.C. actually meant something. New York was a bigger city, but D.C. consistently broke new artists, and because of the large concentration of black folks, it was the place to be.

Videos transformed the music industry. With the emphasis on visuals, videos led to music being more disposable and increasingly aimed at younger people. I was only in my late 20s, and I was starting to feel disconnected. The acts I'd grown up with — The Isley Brothers, The Whispers, and The O'Jays — were not necessarily visual artists. The choreographed dance steps and elaborate routines they put together for live shows didn't transfer well to the small screen.

By 1987, the music had started to change. Up until that point, hip hop was mostly fun and R&B songs told stories of love and romance. But the music industry wanted more sex. Images became racier and stories became increasingly sexual. At the same time, the very concept of having a band was falling apart.

One night, I went to see D Train at The Carter Barron Amphitheatre in Northwest D.C. They came onstage with nothing but four keyboards on stands. They had no drums and no guitars. For most of today's music lovers, seeing a pop act in concert automatically means lip syncing and canned music. But when D Train came out with just keyboards, I was shocked. Where was the *band?* Where was the *music?*

A few years later, I came to work at WKYS and saw Kenny "Babyface" Edmonds sitting in the office; he was about go on the air with Donnie Simpson. At the time, Babyface was in a group called The Deele along with L.A. Reid. We started talking, and I told him about seeing D Train in concert. Babyface was quiet, just nodding his head.

"Everything's changing," he said softly. "Musicians are going to become producers. It's cheaper that way."

Babyface was on the verge of becoming one of the most successful musicians-turned-producers in the history of pop music.

But that night, he seemed to be just as worried as I was about the future of Black music.

My personal future in radio and video seemed to be bright. Nationally, WKYS was in the top 10 for six years, I became the coordinator of music videos for BET and I worked for "Music Video Connection." I bought my own house in Silver Springs, I drove a Saab one year and a BMW the next, and I took exotic vacations to Cancun, London, Paris, and the Caribbean. I truly believed I would be at WKYS until I was old and gray. After six great years, I was beginning to think the station would be like WABC and WMAL, where people worked for 25 years and then retired from radio.

Then in 1988, the Federal Communications Commission (FCC), the governing body for the communications industry, passed a new law that limited ownership of media properties. Companies like NBC were only allowed to have a certain number of radio stations. NBC already owned WRC, which had a news and talk format, so it was WKYS that had to be sold. We got a memo that NBC was going to sell the station, but no one knew who the new owners would be.

NBC would save $15 million dollars in taxes if they sold it to a minority-owned business, which is exactly what they did. Everyone was introduced to the new owners in late 1988. Bertram Lee and Ron Brown, who would go on to become the Secretary of Commerce in the Clinton administration, were partners in a new communications company that had made the purchase. Along with the new General Manager, Skip Finley, they assured us all that nothing was going to change. If this had been 1982 and I'd been fresh from Boston, I might have believed them. But D.C. had trained me well, and I knew bullshit when I smelled it. Their priority was to bust up the union. When they arrived, we were all being paid at the top of the pay scale. Half of the employees were forced out and replaced by lower-paid, less experienced workers.

Ron Brown and Bert Lee took over on a Friday. Skip Finley stayed at the station around the clock that weekend, firing jocks as they came off the air. I had a shift on Sunday, and I went in not knowing what to expect. At the end of my show, I didn't know whether to sign off and say goodbye to my loyal listeners forever or just until the next day. I don't know why I tried to delay the inevitable, but I signed off about 10 minutes early and tried to rush out of the studio. Before I could get to the door, I heard someone yelling my name down the hall. It was Skip Finley.

"I'm sorry Paul, I really wanted to keep you," Skip said. "But Donnie told me to fire you." Everyone had gotten a severance check from NBC after they sold the station. My check was for $72,000, so I wasn't thinking about money when Skip fired me. I was thinking about the white jocks that Donnie kept on while letting me go. What did he say to me on my first night on the air? *As long as I'm here, you'll have a job.* The new owners were keeping Donnie, and they were obviously letting him pick and choose who got fired. So what happened?

I called Donnie as soon as I got home and told him what Skip had said. He was speechless. He stuttered, and then he just said, "Man, you know how it is."

I was angry, frustrated and upset. I still had my gig on "Music Video Connection," and I had nearly six figures in the bank. But I didn't have a plan for the next step in my life. So I did something I'd never done before — I went on a vacation, alone.

Two days after I got fired, I was in Saint Thomas, lying on a raft in the middle of the Caribbean Sea and wondering what I was going to do next. I got a job almost as soon as I returned home. Tony Rose, who had sold ads for WKYS, was now at WDJY, a.k.a. DJ 100. The station was never ranked very highly, and it was more than a step down from WKYS. But Tony arranged a meeting for me and I went, albeit reluctantly. I got the job, and the Program Director wasted no time trying to cut me down to size. He wanted me to adhere to a strict playlist. My days of playing what I wanted were over.

"I know you're a big deal in radio," he said. "But around here we do things differently."

After three weeks, I went home at the end of the day and never went back. I didn't even bother to call to say I'd quit. I told Tony I was out of there, and I guess he relayed the message. I wasn't sure what I was going to do, but I knew I wasn't letting a clueless Program Director tell me how to do my job at a bootleg station with a weak signal and a dirty studio. I thought about looking into working at BET, which had moved into its own studio. Donnie Simpson was my only connection to BET, and it was obvious that he was not in a position to look out for me.

Chapter 5: Being Pimped

I called Cathy Hughes, the owner of WOL, the AM station I'd visited years before. Although she'd since moved into a new building and acquired a new FM station, she was still struggling. Her AM station was frozen in the early '60s. The jocks had names like "The Moon Man" and "The Mo' Betta Man." They talked slick — that smooth, rhyming voice that old school jocks used: *Yeah baby! Call me up anytime. I'm on the line.* Cathy's jocks actually had to pay her something like $15 per shift. To make money, they sold advertising spots to local shops, and they did their own commercials live on the air: *Chicken wings on sale for 49 cents a pound. Come in to Joe's Butcher Shop now!* The audience was made up mostly of cab drivers who drove cars from the late '70s that didn't have FM radio.

Over at WKYS, we used to make jokes about how a radio jock was going to be killed over there because the station was in a terrible neighborhood in Northeast Washington. You'd drive down that street, look up and see the jock in the window while street people were shuffling around below. The only thing the AM station had going for it was Cathy Hughes' morning show. She was politically active, and she had a loyal segment of the black community who tuned in every day.

Even though I didn't listen to her station, I knew who Cathy was. We'd crossed paths at various parties and industry events over the years, and I knew the basics about her background. She was divorced, she'd gotten the AM station as part of the settlement and she had a son, Alfred Liggins, who worked for her but wasn't especially qualified. There was an air of mystery about Cathy. She carried herself like she had a few secrets.

We met in her tiny office at the station. The first thing she said to me made me wonder about her. "All of my employees know to call me *Ms.* Hughes," she said.

I raised an eyebrow. She was only 10 years older than me. I just nodded my head and listened. Her new FM station, Majic 102.3, was located in the basement of the building. This was not NBC. But I needed a job and Cathy was offering one.

She told me that Lee Michaels, a well-known radio consultant, was working with her, and they were looking for a new staff. They had already decided to change over to a new format: Urban Adult Contemporary. The station was going to be what was known as a gold-based format, which meant it would play oldies but goodies, records that were more than 10 years old.

I'd heard of Lee Michaels. He was known for scoring a million-dollar contract as Program Director for Chicago's WBMX. It was the first — and probably the last — such contract for any black radio executive, but I honestly believed he'd sold Cathy and her son Alfred a bunch of wolf tickets. He hadn't done much in radio since his days in Chicago. Now, he was based in San Diego and flying into D.C. once a month or so to check on the station. It seemed strange to me. How was Lee Michaels doing anything for the station from San Diego? And why hadn't his consulting accomplished anything in the past year since Cathy brought him on board? Majic had a zero share in the marketplace — no ranking whatsoever. No one was tuning in to the station.

I listened to Cathy's pitch and remained unimpressed. Finally, she said, "Hey, just come give it a try." I asked her what she was going to pay me. She told me the salary was $18,000 a year. I couldn't do anything but smile. Was she serious? When I left WKYS, I was making $72,000! What she was offering was absolutely nuts! I knew part-time jocks on low-ranked stations that made more than $18,000. Cathy wouldn't negotiate on the salary. "Just come and try it," she said.

I told her I wanted to be Music Director so that I could assist in creating the playlist. She refused. Lee Michaels was handling the music. He would send me the playlist and I would play it. It sounded like what I'd gone through at WDJY, where I'd quit after the Program Director told me I'd have to follow the playlist. I was not excited.

I was still hosting "Music Video Connection," which was consistently Number 1 in its time slot. I wasn't broke — I still had some money in the bank — so I decided to give it a try. I would start in early February doing the 7 p.m. to midnight shift.

On my first day, I came in before my shift started and waited for the jock before me to finish out his show. "Up next," he said, "A Washington, D.C. radio legend…" I didn't feel like a legend as I settled into the booth. The headphones were broken, and as I spoke, I could hear my own voice coming out of one side. I cued up the first song and played it. It wasn't a funky track that described my character, like when I played Sly Stone's "Sex Machine" on my first day at WKYS. It was "Proud Mary" by Ike and Tina Turner. In 1989, the song was more than 15 years old. I knew Cathy Hughes and Lee Michaels wanted to play oldies, but this was ridiculous! No one in D.C. would be jamming to "Proud Mary." I grabbed the playlist and scanned it. There were no records by Deniece Williams or Con Funk Shun, just The Four Tops, The Temptations and other acts from the '50s and '60s. I knew that Majic was going for an Urban Adult format, but this was insane.

I called Cathy Hughes the next day and told her I wasn't coming back. She asked me to come in so we could meet in person. I dressed for a game of tennis and stopped by the station on my way to the tennis court.

"This ain't happening," I told Cathy.

"Why not?" she asked.

"I know this city," I told her. "And I know this market. I just left a Number 1 station. I can't work here for $18,000. As a matter of fact, I couldn't work here for $50,000, because I don't believe in it."

I have to admit, Cathy Hughes listened intently to every word I said in that brief meeting. I told her I didn't know what Lee Michaels was doing, but what they'd come up with was horrible. On top of the corny records they were playing, the station had a bad signal. You could barely hear it in an office building. With a weak signal and a busted playlist, I was through with Majic, and I told Cathy so. Before I left, Cathy asked me what would work for me.

"Play some Luther," I told her. "Play some Earth, Wind & Fire, some Parliament. You can play oldies without playing music for old *people*. Play the old joints that people actually want to hear."

With my tennis racket in my hand, I left. I never expected to hear from Cathy Hughes again.

To my surprise, she called me back the very next day and offered me the job of Program Director, changed my shift to the coveted morning drive and told me I could hire a staff. I was intrigued. The idea of building the station from the ground up was appealing. At WKYS, I'd helped program the station, but I got no credit for it and didn't have the title. Here, I would be Program Director. Still, Cathy was not trying to compensate me for the extra responsibilities. She wanted me to operate as Program Director, manage an entire staff of jocks and have a morning drive shift from 6 to 10 a.m. for $18,000 a year. I couldn't believe she would have the audacity to tack on more job titles and think she didn't have to pay me for it. She even told me that all the jocks I hired, no matter where they came from or how big they were, could only make $18,000 per year.

"I never paid a jock more than $18,000," she told me more than once. And the way she said it let me know she wasn't planning on paying more anytime soon.

I told her I would take the job under one condition: We'd have to work out a system for bonuses. If I brought the ratings up, she'd have to pay me accordingly. She agreed and I quickly called my old boss, Sunny Joe White, to find out what kind of bonus structure I should ask for.

Like all media outlets, radio stations make their money through advertising. The more people you can reach, the more money you can charge advertisers for a spot on your station. A company called Arbitron ranks stations according to the number of listeners each station can claim, which is called their "market share." One share was worth about a million dollars in advertising revenue. Sunny Joe told me to ask for $1500 for every one-tenth of a share that the station went up. That meant that for every million dollars in advertisement revenue I produced for Cathy Hughes, she would owe me $15,000.

"$15,000 for you every time you make her a million," Sunny Joe said. "How could she not go for that?"

Sunny Joe was right. I told Cathy what I wanted, and she agreed. A week after I walked out of the dingy basement on Wisconsin Avenue, I was back again, this time with a new job and the same ridiculous salary, but an incentive — both financial and personal — to make it work.

Lee Michaels flew in soon after I started. I was supposed to answer to him, but I didn't take him seriously. I thought Cathy was wasting her money having him as a consultant, and he knew right away that I wasn't answering to him. He saw me as competition — not a new employee — and that's exactly the way it was. Cathy had hired me, and she was the only person I planned to listen to. I was too cocky to take orders from Lee.

Lee Michaels had a uniform that he never deviated from: He wore a blue suit with a white shirt and a red tie every single day. Hearing him talk about music was like hearing Pee Wee Herman talk about how much he loved gangsta rap. It just didn't feel genuine.

I tolerated Lee during that first meeting. He told me he would be sending me the playlist, and he expected me to adhere it. This was my first taste of how corporate playlists would have a negative impact on radio and the music industry. Having Lee managing the station from across the country made absolutely no sense to me, but Cathy Hughes didn't want her Program Director to have too much power. She wanted people on her payroll that she could control.

As usual, I rebelled against what I thought was unjust and unnecessary. I felt that sticking to computerized playlists was a big mistake. Lee Michaels wanted me to play certain songs at certain times and not change the order because the tempos would be off.

The *only* thing I learned from Lee Michaels was the nuts and bolts of Arbitron and how the country determined how many shares a radio station could claim. I took whatever information I could from Lee Michaels about technology-related subjects and ignored everything else he suggested, especially when it came to music.

The first thing I needed to do as Program Director was to hire staff. At WKYS, I went out of my way to introduce myself to jocks at other stations. I was always loyal to WKYS, but that didn't mean I didn't know jocks on competing stations that I respected. It was from this pool of fellow jocks that I formed my crew.

I hired Bree Taylor, who had been working at WDJY, and put her on middays. She actually took a pay cut to join me, because she believed in what I was trying to do. In less than a month, I had my whole staff in place. The only missing piece was someone for the 7 p.m. to midnight shift. I wanted to hire my boy Bob Thomas, who I'd met when he was a part-timer at WKYS. He had a great voice, a deep baritone that would be perfect for the station. The only problem was that Bob had worked for Cathy years before. She'd called him while he was on the air to let him know he was fired, but that she still expected him to finish out his shift. Bob walked out, cursing Cathy as he left. He didn't think she'd let him work there again, even though it had been years since that happened.

I needed Bob Thomas. It was hard enough trying to find talented jocks who would work for $18,000 a year. But Bob would do it, and he was good. I put his name on the list of people I planned to hire, and Cathy called me into her office right away.

"You want to hire Bob Thomas?!" she yelled. "He walked out on me!"

"Look," I told Cathy. "You're only giving me $18,000 dollars to pay jocks. What do you want me to do? What happened with Bob happened a long time ago. And how are you gonna fire someone while they're still on the air anyway?"

"Are you telling me I'm not going to have trouble out of him and you really need him?" Cathy asked. I said yes. To her credit, Cathy told me I could hire Bob. I couldn't believe it, and neither could Bob when I told him the news.

I kept a young man named Scotty Web, who was working in production when I arrived. Scotty was always popping some kind of pill, but somehow, he was always at work doing his thing. And I liked his energy.

There was one jock, Ron Thompson, who was a terrible on-air personality. He was sterile and his voice was monotone. He should have been a newsman, but he was in a midday slot. I knew he had a wife and three kids, and he was a good man. So I just switched him to a midnight shift. Alfred Liggins, Cathy's son, called me up soon after and told me he sounded terrible and to just fire him. I couldn't do it. Finally, I told Ron to only talk once per hour and just play the music, and he had the nerve to get pissed off. *Why can't I talk? What's up with that?*

I said to him, "Look. Do you want a job? Cause they want me to fire you. You got three kids and a wife. Let your ego go."

Ron did let his ego go, and he stayed. As a matter of fact, he's still there today, working as the Program Director for Cathy Hughes' AM station.

The next thing I had to do was get the music together. I changed the playlist from '50s and '60s music to late '70s and '80s music. I started to add groups like Graham Central Station, The Ohio Players and Earth, Wind & Fire — big groups with tempos that would get listeners excited.

The late '80s were a weak time for R&B radio anyway. Powerhouses like Teddy Pendergrass were fading away. Bobby Brown was replacing Stevie Wonder. Groups like The Commodores that had been the core of the urban format were now defunct. Adults didn't want to hear the heavily sampled and electronic sound of groups like Teddy Riley's Guy and Keith Sweat. They still wanted to hear bands and musicians.

I enlisted Scotty to help me get the music library updated. The station had no music — they were literally borrowing music from the AM station upstairs. Since Majic had no rating and didn't report the songs they were playing to Billboard, no one sent music. None of the record reps I'd dealt with in Boston and at WKYS would return my calls, much less send me music. I ended up bringing in over 400 of my own records to be transferred to the station's carts.

Within a few weeks, I knew the station was going to do well. I was picking the songs and playing the music I wanted to hear: "Boogie Nights" by Heatwave, "Love Is the Message" by MFSB. We were able to play hour-long, commercial-free music, because we didn't have any advertisers. The listeners started to come over. It felt good, even better than at WKYS, because Majic was *my* station. I was in control.

Soon after I arrived, the station sponsored a "Make the Switch" campaign, something most new stations do when they first start out. I had a promotion running every hour urging listeners to tell us why they made the switch. We played their responses on the air:

I made the switch 'cause y'all played my jam by Heatwave!

I made the switch because I love AWB!

And then there was my personal favorite:

I made the switch 'cause Donnie Simpson talks too much!

I got a kick out of hearing the listeners talk about the station that dumped me. Donnie *did* talk too much on his morning drive show. I thought that even when I worked there, and now, my own listeners confirmed it. On my morning show, I played music. My slogan was: *While they're talking...we're jamming.*

Every station has an outro, a bit of dialogue that plays at the end of every commercial break. The outro at Majic was: "We're listening to you." I intended to keep it that way. Having listeners talking up Majic was better advertising than we could ever buy.

Lee Michaels sent his playlist weekly. I filed it in the computer and played whatever I wanted. He would complain whenever he was in town, but the research showed that the station was improving week by week, so he couldn't say much. Cathy was happy, and she told me I was doing a great job. If she really wanted me to follow Lee Michaels' playlists, she would have said so. She didn't.

I worked harder at Majic than I'd ever worked at any job. I was responsible for managing my staff and handling payroll for them, and I controlled all the music. I had no secretary and no assistant. I practically lived in the station. I'd wake up in the morning, get to the station around 5:30 a.m. and do my show from 6 a.m. to 10 a.m. It was just me with my news guy, DeNorris Miles, and back then I was lucky to have a separate news guy. Today, you'd be hard-pressed to find a morning show with just one person on it, but in the '80s, station owners didn't want to pay one jock, much less a crew of people.

I was working hard, but I wasn't sure if it would show in the ratings. The station still had a weak signal. No matter how good the music was, if people couldn't hear it, they wouldn't tune in. Plus, Cathy refused to pay for advertisements, so we had to rely on word of mouth. I was hoping we would at least go up to a .5 share, which would mean we'd be worth $500,000 in ad revenue. I wanted us to do well, and I knew my bonuses depended on it. Making $18,000 a year was not going to pay my bills. I needed a nice bonus.

Arbitron puts out four books per year. The first rating came out in April, after I had been at the station for three months. I was dying to find out how we'd done, but Cathy couldn't afford the six-figure price to receive the Arbitron figures. I got a phone call from Alice Jones, a former co-worker, who sold advertisements for WKYS. In three months, Majic had gone from a zero share to a .9 share. I was ecstatic. By the time I got to Cathy, she'd already heard the news, and she was happy too. A .9 share meant that she could sell $900,000 in ad revenue. It also meant that she owed me $1,500 for every tenth of a share increase. My bonus would be $13,500. Cathy wrote me a check for $7,000 that week. The remainder was included in my next paycheck.

Everyone was happy. I was making money, the station was making money and I'd even managed to get bonuses for my jocks. They were each getting $500 for every three-tenths we went up in the first ratings cycle. I'd already told Cathy that each jock should get $1000 if numbers continued to improve. She agreed. Soon after the numbers came out, I got a call from writer and radio host Walt "Baby" Love, who was writing a story about the radio station and its rise. He interviewed me, and I submitted a sample playlist to include in his story. He also interviewed Cathy, who talked about how happy she was with the improvements. Walt did not ask to interview Lee Michaels, and I did not mention his name. Later, I heard that Lee was upset that he was not interviewed.

In preparation for the next ratings book, I continued loading up the library with good music. Lee Michaels told me to keep the library small and play the best 250 songs. I told him there were more songs out there that people wanted to hear. They didn't want to hear the same 250 songs when they tuned in. Why not play the best 850 songs?

When I came to Majic, they had only eight songs carted up and ready to play. Within six months, we had 1200 songs. We played the hit records every five to six hours, so our listeners wouldn't get tired of them. We spread out the oldies so that you could tune in for months and never hear the same oldie twice. I made sure we had lots of good music in our library.

After the first six months, artists started to visit the station. I sat a foot away from Barry White in that dingy basement, awestruck that the "Maestro" was on my show. I interviewed Debbie Allen, who was promoting a local play in the area. We also had artists like Kashif and Jeffrey Osborne. We didn't always have the most popular artists, but I appreciated the artists who stopped by. It was an improvement over being completely ignored. Record reps started to return my calls, and record labels started sending music to the station. Eventually, I was having music meetings and reps were coming in to pitch new music to me.

When the new ratings came out, we *still* weren't subscribing to Arbitron, so I didn't have the information right away. But I knew it had to be good. In the streets, I heard Majic everywhere, coming out of cars, barbershops and restaurants. My boy Tony Rose called me with the advances, and it was an incredible jump. We went from a .9 share to 2.9 shares. That meant in six months, I'd taken Majic from making nothing to making nearly $3 million dollars in revenue. And I'd done it *my* way. Not Lee Michaels' way, not Cathy Hughes' way, and certainly not Alfred Liggins' way. It was the best time in my life. I was building a station from the ground up.

Even though Cathy wouldn't buy billboards, we still made it happen. While WKYS was giving away Thunderbirds and Cadillacs, we were giving away Chevy Geos. With the new ratings out, Cathy owed me $20,000 in bonuses. She'd recently bought a new car and moved from an apartment to a house. The money was rolling in, but Cathy was sticking her finger in the funnel on the payroll side. She gave me $7,000 dollars up front. Then she told me the rest would be financed throughout my salary for the rest of the year. I was not happy. This wasn't the arrangement we'd made. I wanted my bonus up front, the same way she'd paid it during the first rating period. She wasn't getting her money from advertisers *financed* over a year's time. Why was she reneging on me?

It hurt. Not just because I needed the money, which I did, but also because I felt like Cathy Hughes was unprincipled. I had gained 25 pounds in six months spending most of my time working in that dank station. I'd only leave to go across the street to grab food from a greasy Korean diner. Cathy knew how hard I was working. She knew my efforts had paid off for her in a big way. The idea that she would not honor our agreement because she didn't want to part with money left me feeling disillusioned and deflated.

Things got worse when I received a memo from Cathy's son about Herb Alpert, who was the "A" in A&M Records. He was also a musician who played the trumpet and was best known for his instrumental "Rise," which won a Grammy in 1979. Herb had bought advertisements on the station. Cathy and her son were excited about getting money from a record label. They were used to scraping around trading advertisements for services when they couldn't get cash, but those checks from the label were fat and as good as cold hard cash.

In exchange for A&M ads, Alfred Liggins said that Majic would play "Rise" at least 30 times per week. This was straight-up payola, and it was illegal. To make matters worse, Alfred Liggins spelled it out in a memo that went around the office stating that the station had entered into an agreement with Herb Alpert and that we were to play the song 30 times per week. I couldn't believe Alfred would be naive enough to agree to that and much worse, to put it in *writing*. The subject line may as well have been: Corporate Payola.

Between being swindled out of my upfront bonus by Cathy and Alfred's clueless behavior, I was growing weary, and I begin to pull away. I still did my job, but I didn't spend every waking moment at the station. I started going to Pizzeria Uno with Lauren, my work buddy. I went home at a decent hour and did just enough to earn my paltry paycheck. Cathy would upbraid me occasionally, asking me why I wasn't staying late. She had nerve. I picked up my tennis racket and started playing again. Cathy's tightfisted nature became more and more apparent. I looked around, and I didn't like what I saw. I was loaning jocks money week after week because they couldn't survive on $18,000 a year.

At WKYS, working in radio was a step up from working a regular job as a teacher or a postman. It was like television — a glamorous career, not just a grind. But everyone who worked for Cathy Hughes was barely making it. No one owned a house. They were all renting. They didn't even have health benefits. The part-time jocks were making $10 an hour for a four-hour shift. I often fudged the timesheets to give them an eight-hour day instead. It was the least I could do.

Cathy wasn't trying to come up off of any cash for her staff. She would trade advertising spots with a local mechanic and offer repairs and oil changes to her staff. I wasn't letting some no-name mechanic touch my car. The station had cost her $8 million dollars. Cathy was on track to make her money back in less than a year. Why wouldn't she want to compensate her employees properly?

I continued to do my job well, but I did not love it. In the fall, I attended an annual Music Conference in Atlantic City. Record reps and radio executives wanted to talk to me about what I had accomplished at Majic. I felt good knowing that my peers were recognizing my hard work, but my confidence in the company was failing. Cathy Hughes would call me at home and ask why a certain record was on the air or why there was a few seconds of dead air. She'd even call me and tell me to play a certain record while she was out with friends so she could show off.

Even though I wasn't working day and night like I did at the beginning, when it was time for the third rating book to come out, I knew we were going to do well. The station was everywhere. Dimensions Unlimited, a popular concert promotion company, had always teamed up with WHUR to promote shows. But that year, they approached Majic. That was proof that we were the station to beat.

In October of 1989, the numbers came out, and we went up from 2.9 shares to 4.6 shares. The stations we competed against posted lower numbers. This meant that not only were we bringing in new listeners, we were also luring them away from our competition. When the news came out, I felt like Cathy owed me the world. Honestly, I still feel that way. She probably thinks they would have gotten it done one way or the other. But Majic was in operation for a year before I came on board with no success.

With the increase in the ratings, Cathy now owed me lots of money. I didn't want to hear anything about financing or anything else. I just wanted my money — all of it. I loved what I had done for the station, but I needed to work somewhere I would be paid what I was worth. Even with my bonuses, I was barely making what I would have as just an on-air jock at another station. At Majic, I was acting as Program Director, on-air jock, and Music Director, all without an assistant or any help.

As the year came to a close, I planned a much-needed vacation. I was attending a wedding in London around Christmas and then spending New Year's Eve in Paris. My friends were going on to Switzerland to ski, but I decided to fly back home from Paris. I'd worked out my vacation with Alfred Liggins and Lee Michaels, and even though I had issues with the station, I didn't want to be away too long. I flew back into Dulles airport on the first day of the year.

It was not only a new day and a new month, but also a new decade. It was snowing when the plane landed, and I felt good. I was rested and relaxed, and ready to get back to work.

I got my Saab from the airport and tuned in to Majic for the ride home. My boy Bob Thomas was on the air. I wanted to wish him a Happy New Year, so I called in from my car phone when he went to commercial.

"There are memos all over the station," Bob told me. "You're not allowed in here. Paul, your stuff is all locked away. I heard there's a Western Union waiting for you at your house. These mu'fuckas is getting rid of you!"

I drove home in a furious daze. All I could think was: *No they didn't!* I knew I was supposed to work on a new contract with Cathy because she didn't want to continue paying me bonuses, but I was sure my job would be secure. I pulled into the garage of my condo and went to the front desk. There was a cute Indian girl working there who I spoke to from time to time. She was happy to see me, giving me a cheerful "Welcome back!" when I came up to get my mail. I tried to be cordial, but all I could think about was the yellow Western Union envelope sticking out of my mail. I headed for the elevator and opened it while I waited.

"Paul Porter: Your services are no longer needed at WMMJ. Please contact Lee Michaels for further details. –Cathy Hughes."

Cathy made sure she wouldn't have to pay me the last bonus owed to me. She fired me two weeks before the next ratings would come out. I went to my apartment, rolled a huge joint and sat on my couch. Bob Thomas called when he got in from his shift. He told me they already had a replacement for me and said Lee Michaels had been scheming to get me out because I'd been getting all the credit for revitalizing the station. I called my old friends and co-workers. Sunny Joe cursed me out for working without a contract. I tried to explain to him that she didn't do contracts. All I had was her word, which, as it turned out, didn't mean a thing.

Cathy Hughes dodged my calls for the next few days and then told me I could come in to collect my things. When I got there,

Conan, a beefy jock from the AM station, was in the lobby in case I decided to get wild. I made my way to Cathy's office, and she handed me a severance check for $800. I just looked at the check and then looked at her.

"Paul, you went AWOL," she said, referring to my vacation.

"What are you talking about? Everyone knew my plans."

Cathy let that one go. She knew it didn't make sense, but she had to rationalize her reasons for firing me.

"You're a great programmer and a great jock," she said. "But you're not a company man. You were fighting to get the jocks more money. That's why I had to let you go."

"You just didn't want to pay me," I said.

Her son came into the office and looked like he was about to say something to me.

"Get out of my face," I told him. He left the office.

Scotty helped me pack up that chapter of my life into my Saab. And just like that, the Majic was gone. For the next five years, I never let the dial on my radio rest on Majic 102.3 FM. I'd lost more than just a job; I'd lost a part of myself. Working at Majic was a one-of-a-kind experience, one I knew I might never have again. In broadcasting, when you get the opportunity to start a station from scratch — and you're actually successful — that's a career highlight. I've had low points in my life, but being fired from Majic was something different. It was all about money, and I felt like I'd been pimped.

Chapter 6: Now I See It

Fortunately, I still had my weekend job at "Music Video Connection." I needed time to think about my next steps. I assumed I would have to leave D.C.; I felt like I'd worked at just about every urban radio station in the city. I thought about trying to get a job at a station in New York, but I was too depressed to look for work.

Just two weeks after I left Majic, my producer at "Music Video Connection" gave me a message that Lydia Cole, a Vice President at BET, had called the station asking for me. Lydia wanted to know if I would be interested in substituting for Donnie Simpson on one of the channel's highest-rated shows, "Video Soul."

BET had stepped up its game since those early days when Donnie first took me to the studio Bob Johnson was renting. They'd moved into their own studios off New York Avenue, and the station was broadcast in millions of homes. I now watched BET on a regular basis. Although the station didn't air after 10 o'clock, they still featured a few good shows, and "Video Soul" was one of them. I was used to seeing Donnie on the show, sitting on a couch with a television right next to him that displayed his picture onscreen. It seemed a little strange that even though we didn't speak anymore, fate was pushing me in his direction.

The following Monday, I was sitting on that familiar couch, getting ready to read the teleprompter. It felt strange. Here I was sitting on Donnie's couch, where he'd interviewed the who's who of black entertainment. Although I was now hosting the show, his image was still on the TV screen. A year had passed since I'd left WKYS, and I was not bitter about being fired. All in all, I knew Donnie had done a lot for me.

My experience doing "Fresh" and "Music Video Connection" had made me as comfortable being on television as I was on radio. That day, I looked the part. I'd gone to Hugo Boss and bought a purple jacket and complemented it with a black shirt and dress slacks. I spent $1200 for my ensemble to do a job that was paying $250. I invested in my appearance, and it paid off. When the taping was complete, I received lots of compliments. Lydia Cole assured me that I'd done a great job. I tried to introduce a hip, vibrant flair to the show, and the producers took note. Later that week, the producer of "Video Soul" called me back in; she wanted to hire me to do voice-overs.

It's part of the BET legend that Bob Johnson took pride in keeping costs low. Instead of hiring "live" talent, which would include makeup and styling costs, he would produce shows that required voice-over announcers to introduce the videos. "Video Soul" was one of the few shows that actually had a real host. I filled in for Donnie once more on "Video Soul," then I began doing voice-overs for "Video Vibrations," a midday video show, and "Midnight Love," a late-night show featuring videos of love songs. For each show, I made $250. Both shows came on five times per week. The pay was generous, and the work was easy. I didn't do the voice-overs in real time; I would just pre-record a quick line or two for the beginning of the show: *Welcome to Midnight Love. This is the Captain, Paul Porter. And here is the new one from Johnny Gill.*

Then I would record a few more announcements to run before and after commercials. This was similar to what I did on radio, except it was better because I didn't have to sit through each video. It would take me less than an hour to record everything needed for a show. Within a month, BET added a third show, "Soft Note." I was now making $750 *per day* for less than two hours of work.

Although I was paid well, the full-time employees at BET were making nominal wages, and they were not treated very well. The producers and directors were making salaries in the low $20,000s with no health benefits, and BET's corporate culture was like some twisted version of Jim Crow segregation. Only upper management was allowed to use the front doors of the BET complex; everyone else was expected to enter and exit through the back doors of the studio.

There were a lot of legendary BET personalities working there at the time, including Angela Stribling, Sherry Carter, and Melvin Lindsey. I didn't hang out with any of the employees there. I'd walk into the station using the front door, record my lines and leave. I wasn't vying for Employee of The Month. After all, I was still in shock over what had happened at Majic. In my leisure time, I chased women and had fun.

The truth is, I still wanted to be on the radio airwaves. My work at BET was paying well, but I wasn't being challenged. They hired me because I had a deep voice and experience. I still thought about Majic, and it hurt. The money from BET just helped to chase my blues away.

After a few months at BET, Lydia Cole hired me as a Music Video Consultant. They wanted input from someone who knew music to help determine what videos they should play. I would go in two or three times a week and watch all the videos that came in. Then, we would all vote on which videos should be added to the playlist.

Sometimes we had to turn down videos simply because of the low-quality images. Also, BET had its own set of standards; for example, they wouldn't show alcohol or guns, so we blurred out anything offensive or asked the label to edit the video accordingly. The hard edge of hip hop was becoming more and more popular, and it showed in the types of videos that were being sent to the station. Lydia Cole was a mother and a concerned broadcaster — she wouldn't allow just anything to be aired on BET. Lydia and Senior Producer Verna Dickerson wanted to set a high standard, and they fought to maintain it.

Nevertheless, because of pressure from the sales team, BET played just about everything that was sent to the station. Bad videos might be on what we called "lunar rotation" and get played just once a week. These videos ranged from regional one-hit wonders to independent artists with no major label backing. Back then, BET needed the artists' content as much as the artists needed the exposure. The end result was that the programming on BET was lackluster at best. There were too many low-grade videos.

I settled into my new routine, and by the time 1990 came to a close, I'd taken on another job as the Assistant Music Director for Howard University-owned WHUR. After years of being a strong force in Black radio, WHUR was going through a rough period with terrible ratings. I had a midday shift from 10 a.m. to 3 p.m., and I met with the Program Director once a week to talk about new music. The job paid $60,000 a year. Between this job and the money I was making at BET and as the host of "Music Video Connection," I was clearing six figures.

My bank account was full, but my soul was empty. I didn't know where I really wanted to be, so I accepted opportunities as they came to me without much thought as to where they would lead. I had no cause, no mission, no plan and no direction. I just wanted to be paid and laid. During my early years at BET, that's exactly what I got. It's no coincidence that the music at the time didn't inspire me to chase anything more than money and women.

In the early '90s, Black music began to take on an overtly sexual tone, and the videos took it even further. There was "Freak Me" by Silk, "Baby Got Back" by Sir Mix-a-Lot, "Humpin' Around" by Bobby Brown and, of course, "Rump Shaker" by Teddy Riley's Wreckx-n-Effect. Anyone who came of age in the early '90s remembers the video for "Rump Shaker" as one of the first T&A videos to get major airtime on BET. The video was set on a beach, and every woman was splashing around in skimpy bathing suits. It sounds tame now, but in the early '90s it was just short of scandalous, so much so that it was banned by MTV. That video signaled a real change in the music industry.

The video was no longer a marketing device for a record, and it wasn't just a commercial to make you like a song. Music videos were becoming just as important — if not more important — than the songs themselves. I never heard people say, "Did you hear that new song 'Rump Shaker' by Wreckx-n-Effect?" Everyone talked about the video. Today, no one can recall who was in the group besides Teddy Riley, but anyone who had access to cable in 1992 still remembers that video.

Meanwhile, R&B boy bands like Jodeci and Boyz II Men ran with Teddy Riley's style of "new jack swing." I could see that urban music was changing forever. When Snoop Doggy Dogg released *Doggystyle* in November of 1993, I knew he was putting the final nail in the coffin of Black music as I knew it.

By the mid-'90s, there were severe budget cutbacks at BET. My $250 rate was being cut in half, and the popularity of MTV's "The Box" had the executives at BET nervous. MTV, which had originally refused to showcase black artists, now had exclusivity contracts to prevent the biggest acts from airing on BET for the first 30 days after the release of their videos. BET reacted by boycotting all of the artists on certain record labels, including Sony and Jive, who continued to allow MTV to have exclusivity. The executives at BET also decided to clean house and attempt to reel in younger viewers who wanted to hear more hip hop and modern R&B. Donnie Simpson was slowly being phased out, and one of his first replacements was a sad testament to just how clueless BET could be when it came to hiring on-air talent.

Brett Walker, a six-foot-four former model from New Jersey, was brought in to host a show called "In Your Ear." Brett was a nice enough guy off the air, but he had zero personality and no experience in television. He looked good, but he just wasn't a professional announcer. Brett's first assignment was to interview Boyz II Men for "In Your Ear." He choked on-air and froze up, completely star struck and unable to read the teleprompter. After a few fruitless takes, the producer had to put a transmitter in his ear so that he could have questions and dialogue pumped to him. It was bad. But Brett really placed himself into the hall of shame when his show went on location to the set of *The Bodyguard* to interview Whitney Houston.

Whitney's handlers brought her outside her trailer to talk with Brett about the movie. After the Boyz II Men fiasco, you'd think BET would have prepared questions for Brett. But for some reason, he was left to his own devices. Brett asked Whitney how filming on the movie was going, and Whitney smiled and said it was going great. Then, he asked her if she was planning to record any songs for the movie soundtrack. That question quickly wiped the smile off Whitney's pretty face.

"I Will Always Love You," the lead single from the soundtrack to *The Bodyguard,* had been released six weeks before and was the Number 1 song in the country. You heard the song everywhere you went, and the video was in heavy rotation on BET. In addition, Whitney had recorded half a dozen other songs that appeared on the soundtrack, which exploded even before the movie finished filming. Whitney ripped her microphone off and walked back to her trailer without saying another word to Brett. That was the beginning and the end of Brett Walker's career.

It made me wonder if BET had the right idea. Did it make sense to cater to a younger crowd using inexperienced talent with little knowledge of music? Brett had been working as a porter at the Newark Airport when a BET executive discovered him. He was clearly unqualified, and it seemed as if BET was sacrificing professional standards for a quick fix of credibility with youth culture. They also enlisted another young host, Madelyne Woods, who was immortalized in A Tribe Called Quest's song "Electric Relaxation": *"Not to come across as a thug or a hood/But hon, you got the goods, like Madelyne Woods."*

It wasn't until Bob Johnson came up with BET on Wheels not long after I arrived that I began to notice how the music was affecting Black culture. BET on Wheels was Bob's plan to connect to youth culture nationwide. He'd created a soundstage inside of an 18-wheeler that was decorated with BET's bold black and gold star logo, and the goal was to tour cities nationwide so that young people could experience a live version of the channel, with artists performing in various cities. Of course, none of the multiplatinum acts like Mary J. Blige, Wu-Tang Clan, Xscape, and Jodeci were paid for their performances. At that time, artists performed for BET for free...*or else.*

I traveled with BET on Wheels all across the country: Los Angeles, Tulsa, Chicago, and Atlanta. Prior to each event, I would meet with teenagers from the area and hosted small forums. It was at one of these forums in Tulsa that I noticed firsthand how the images in music videos were affecting the youth.

There was a young man in the front of the crowd barely hiding a shiny black revolver in his pants. He boasted that the streets he lived on were tough and spat out the lyrics to a song by rap group Onyx that was prominent on the network. In their most popular song, "Throw Ya Gunz," rapper Sticky Fingaz famously screamed: "*I hate your fuckin guts, and I hope that you die/Sticky Fingaz' my name, and my life is a lie/Plus I'm having a bad day, so stay out of my way/And we're the pistol packing people, so you better obey/Just in the nick of time, I commit the perfect crime ... And what's mines is mines, and what's yours is mine/Don't fuckin blink or I'ma rob yo' ass blind.*"

This young man in Tulsa knew nothing about life on the streets of Queens, N.Y., where the young men from Onyx got their start. I'm sure his life was tough. But his mannerisms, the way he dressed, the way he carried himself, everything down to the words falling out of his mouth came courtesy of a rap group he saw perform every day at the station I worked for. I felt a hint of something wrong, but I didn't show it. Tulsa was just a pit stop. I wouldn't have to deal with that young man after the soundstage pulled off for the next city. I was making money, and I had a great job. I wasn't trying to change the world. I was having too many good times in D.C. for my moral compass to be pointed in the right direction. The reps could still be counted on to throw the wildest parties imaginable, financed by record labels that wanted to keep industry folks happy. I was too cocky and selfish to think about anything but myself and what was immediately next for me. But the image of a Midwestern young man desperately looking for an identity in a cartoonish rap group would haunt me.

On the weekends, I played basketball with my old friend Neville, who rented out the court at his old high school. After one game, he told me that Wendy Williams, a jock who'd relocated to D.C. after working at a small station in the Virgin Islands, wanted to meet up with me. I'd met Wendy a few times before at industry functions. She talked like a Valley Girl, which I thought was cute, but she wasn't particularly my type. This was pre-surgery Wendy Williams — big boned, small breasts. But she had solid, thick legs like a dancer. I called her up and we set up a time to hook up that weekend.

Wendy was working for Cathy Hughes at WOL. Neville, who worked there, had heard her tape and brought her on. He'd even found a place for her to live. Wendy had been a student at Northeastern University a few years after I left, and she'd worked at WRBB. By then, I was a legend in Boston. I was the one who'd gone on to work at NBC, which was as big as you could get in radio. At that point, Wendy was probably impressed by my career, but I wasn't. I filled in on "Video Soul" for an entire summer while Donnie went on vacation, and I was surprised to be hounded for autographs when I traveled to Atlanta for a show. But working at BET was a job; I didn't see it as a career. I didn't *feel* the music.

Although BET's Bob Johnson is a black man and a businessman, he is not a "race man." Even Cathy Hughes, as cheap as she was, provided the illusion of caring for black people and running a family-like business. But BET was growing by leaps and bounds every year, and as Bob Johnson got richer, his staff became more and more disillusioned. He took the company public in 1991 and was promptly sued by some employees who said they were cheated out of their share. He was forced to pay $1.2 million in compensation.

The bigger BET became, the more Bob Johnson's shady side was revealed. He fired his own sister, one of the first employees of BET. She later sued him and was awarded $1 million dollars. Although Johnson had originally been quoted as saying he wanted BET to be a place for positive African-American images, he gave that up when he saw what videos like "Rump Shaker" could do for his own bottom line. It always seemed to me that in order for Bob Johnson to make you a Vice President at BET, you had to be either a short, non-threatening male or a tall, curvaceous woman. I was neither, so I knew my future with the company was limited.

From 1990 to 1997, I was "the voice" of BET. I did voice-overs for several shows and I helped Lydia program the channel. During my tenure, I never had more than a 30-second conversation with Bob Johnson. One year, he did invite me to a Christmas party at his house. I was instructed to wear a suit and not bring anyone with me. The only other talent who attended the party was Ed Gordon, who did news, and Sherry Carter, the newest jock for "Video Soul." Bob Johnson lived off Connecticut Avenue in Northwest D.C. in a neighborhood surrounded by redwood trees. The house was beautiful and the party was nice. But I felt on edge around Bob and his wife. The people who worked on the business side called him Bob, while the talent and the creative people called him Mr. Johnson. He was stuffy and corporate. He didn't seem like the type you could just walk up to and start a conversation with.

Bob Johnson got his point across very clearly a few years later during a meeting in a downtown D.C. hotel. The meeting was called to explain the state of the company, but it was also a chance for Bob and his Executive VP, Jeff Lee, to explain why they weren't supporting the employee's efforts to become unionized. I was a contracted employee, so I wouldn't benefit from a union, but I went to the meeting anyway to see what they had to say. The results were disheartening.

"You do not have shackles on your feet," Jeff Lee told a crowd of 300 BET employees. "If you don't want to work here, go get a job at the Discovery Channel."

Bob Johnson came to the microphone after Lee. "I didn't start this company for any of you," he said. "I started this company to support my family. Think of BET as a steppingstone for you. When you want to make more money, move on."

The crowd was stunned. Bob Johnson was a businessman, not a social activist. The main thing I didn't like was the fact that he'd changed the game plan when it was convenient for him. He got BET into millions of homes with videos and a variety of shows like "Lead Story," "Teen Summit," and news shows with Ed Gordon and Tavis Smiley. But as soon as it was time to take his company public, he cut the shows that needed real budgets and converted BET to nothing more than a music video station. Even the comedians on the stand-up comedy show "Comic View" were paid a flat fee of $150. I won't judge Bob Johnson for his business practices, but that doesn't mean I have to like how his choices impacted Black culture.

By the time 2 Live Crew's indecency trial ended, urban music had spiraled out of control. As a result, the U.S. Senate held a hearing on song lyrics. Major record companies responded by voluntarily agreeing to place stickers on albums that contained explicit lyrics. Two things were happening at the same time: Music was becoming more and more suggestive and obscene, and parental advisory stickers had labeled hip hop almost exclusively as dangerous music. Unfortunately, even acts that were relatively clean were given a warning label. Rap music became synonymous with a black and white sticker on the bottom right corner of a CD, tape or record cover. Meanwhile, stations like BET became a forum for gangsta rappers to showcase their vulgarity. The T&A videos could now be seen all day and half the night, as BET slowly started to increase their on-air hours.

By this time, D.C. had become stagnant for me. My salary was cut in half, and the music no longer excited me. My decision to leave was sealed when I lost my girlfriend in a tragic plane crash. I stayed with her mother for a month after the accident, helping her to adjust. Soon, my girlfriend's mother moved to New York, and I went up for a visit.

While in New York City, I visited WQHT HOT 97 and spoke to DJ Bugsy. He told me that the legendary Frankie Crocker, a mainstay at WBLS, was looking for someone to fill in for him. I made some calls, and within weeks, I was moving to New York City to work for one of the most notable names in the history of Black radio.

Little did I know that everything I had been shielded from was about to be exposed in full view. At BET, I'd questioned some of the music and videos Jeff Lee told us to play, but nothing appeared to be an out-and-out scandal. Now, I'd see payola up close and personal, and this illegal behavior would come from a jock I'd always idolized: Frankie Crocker.

"You sound good man," Frankie Crocker said to me. "You sound real good."

For anyone in the radio business, hearing these words from Frankie Crocker was the equivalent of Michael Jordan saying you had skills on the basketball court. Frankie Crocker wasn't just any old radio jock. He was a star and a celebrity in his own right.

I'd heard lots of scandalous stories about Frankie, but as I sat in his office on the 40th Floor of 3 Park Avenue, overlooking the Hudson River, all I could think about was the fact that I was being interviewed by the man whose voice I emulated. Any black person who grew up in New York in the '70s and '80s — and lots of white ones too — knew about the "Chief Rocker" Frankie Crocker. He had the most recognizable voice on radio for many years.

In person, this man was cool and smooth, just like he was on the radio. Frankie heard my tape and wanted me to start a new shift on Saturdays. I was looking forward to the opportunity. There was only one catch: I couldn't identify myself on the radio. Frankie thought I sounded so much like him that I could do a Saturday show using all of his drops and promos and just pretend to be him, including playing his well-known close-out song, "Moody's Mood for Love." It sounds insane, but at the time I was actually flattered that Frankie thought I was good enough to pretend to be him.

The one thing that freaked me out about Frankie was that he never made eye contact with me. Throughout our entire meeting, he never looked at me. He would talk, sounding exactly as he did on the radio, and his eyes would be everywhere, except on me.

Frankie had me sit in with another jock who I'd known since my days in D.C. so I could learn the ropes. It felt good to be back in radio, in the Number 1 radio market in the country. But 1996 was going to bring more changes to radio than I'd experienced during my entire career. And those changes would have trickle-down effects that would be impossible to reverse.

When I slid into my chair for my first shift at WBLS, something was different. This was not the kind of studio I was used to. Instead of the familiar carts of music, there was only an on-air button and a button to start the music. The digital era had come to radio, and there was no actual music in the studio. For me, being able to queue up the music and see the song titles and album covers at every other station I'd worked at made a difference. That empty studio made me feel disconnected. Without the physical music in hand, I didn't know what a new artist looked like or if an old group had changed a member or two. I didn't know C+C Music Factory was using an imposter in place of Martha Wash. I couldn't see the album, although we were playing the song. Gone were the days when I could tell the listeners who played the bass on a particular record after it ended. Now even radio jocks had to watch videos if they wanted to know who was who.

After my first shift, I got a call from Hal Jackson, who was on the air right before me. He was one of the owners of the station and was a well-respected giant in the industry. Hal asked me why I never said my name on my shift.

"Frankie told me not to," I replied. "He said to just run the show like I'm filling in for him."

Hal Jackson was livid. "Paul," he said, "you're *not* filling in for him. Frankie doesn't even have a show on Saturdays! He can't just have you do a Frankie Crocker show any day of the week!"

I didn't know how to respond to Hal. I knew he was right, but Frankie had hired me and I didn't question his instructions.

I was working at WBLS part-time, so I had plenty of time to continue my pursuit of voice-over work. A few labels had hired me to do voice-overs for upcoming albums for Brian McKnight and Will Downing, and I knew how lucrative the work could be. When I was done with BET for the week, I'd drive up to NYC, do my radio show on Saturday and then spend Monday and Tuesday auditioning for voice-over work in New York.

Years before, I'd met the actor Adolph Caesar, famous for his roles in "A Soldier's Story" and "The Color Purple." I played basketball at Northeastern with his nephew, and I briefly dated his niece. Although Uncle Adolph, as I called him, had been nominated for an Academy Award and a Golden Globe for "A Soldier's Story," his fortune had been made as a voice-over artist. He was the voice of the United Negro College Fund's *"Because a mind is a terrible thing to waste"* slogan, and he was the original voice of Hotwing in the animated series "Silverhawks."

"Radio?" he would say to me. "You need to be doing voice-overs. Your problem is you just want some sex. Radio will get you some sex, but there ain't no money in radio."

I never forgot what Uncle Adolph told me, and years after he died, I was in Manhattan, trying to follow his advice. With voice-overs, the work is in getting the work. On average, a voice-over announcer will go to 40 auditions before getting a job. During my first year, I got lucky. I got a national spot for AT&T's "It's All Within Your Reach" campaign. For the AT&T spot alone, I made thousands of dollars. I received $125 every time the commercial ran on any station, and since it was a national spot, sometimes it would run 20 times per day on each station.

Meanwhile, at WBLS, all of the jocks had strict instructions to play "Ascension (Don't Ever Wonder)" by Maxwell. It was a good song, and it fit WBLS's format, but I quickly figured out that something was wrong. We were playing the song over and over. Frankie called it his "hit pick," but the amount of play it got on the station bordered on outrageous. Not only were we required to play it up to three times during our shift, we had to "front sell it" and "back sell it." That meant that before the song came on, we had to give it a special introduction like: "And now, a WBLS exclusive, the new joint by Maxwell, 'Ascension,' on 107.5 WBLS." Then, when the song ended, we'd say: "That was an exclusive from a new artist, Maxwell."

WBLS did have an exclusive — because no other radio station in the country was playing it. Maxwell was signed to Columbia

Records, and the label rep was Ken Wilson, who was known as a "by any means necessary" kind of guy. He did whatever he had to do to get a song on the radio, and it became crystal clear to me that he was paying Frankie to get the song on WBLS.

It was during this time that I began to see how payola really worked. I always knew it existed, but I'd never really seen it up close. I wasn't surprised; I was disappointed. Even after the stories I'd heard about Frankie getting his legs broken after he took money for playing a record that never made it to the radio, I didn't want to think he'd be that blatant about playing a song so frequently. Eventually, other stations started to play the song, and Maxwell's debut album was a rousing success. The only saving grace was that the song was actually good. Frankie had advised Ken to change the original single he was pushing and chose "Ascension" as the song he thought could break through. Frankie chose right. The record was certified gold, it peaked in the Top 10 on Billboard's R&B songs and it reached the Top 40 on the Hot 100 list.

Frankie's payola schemes were just one part of the problem with the playlist at WBLS. Hip hop was slowly taking over, courtesy of Sean "Puffy" Combs and his Bad Boy era, and the resurgence of the West Coast hip-hop sounds of Dr. Dre, Snoop Dogg, and Tupac. WBLS was floundering, and the playlist was all over the place. It was Frankie's job as Program Director to give the station direction, but he wasn't doing it well. At industry parties, I'd hear friends in the business talk about how bad the station sounded. It was true — there would be an O'Jays song on one minute and Biggie's "Mo Money, Mo Problems" the next. There was no rhyme or reason to what was being played on WBLS.

This was Frankie's fourth go-round at the station. The Sutton family, who co-owned the station, had booted him out and brought him back many times over the years. When I came on board, Pierre Sutton, nephew of founder Percy Sutton, was serving as General Manager. He was ineffective and weird, always trying to get into everyone's personal lives. Soon after I arrived at WBLS, he called me into his office.

"Hey, I hear you know my ex-wife," he said.

Immediately, I felt uncomfortable. I *did* know his ex-wife. I'd had a crazy crush on her in college.

"You can have her now if you want," he continued with a laugh.

I laughed too, but it was a mask to hide the fact that I thought he was creepy and inappropriate. Pierre was my boss, the General Manager of the radio station, and the first thing he said to me was not "Welcome to WBLS," but rather, "you can have my ex-wife"? His behavior was as unprofessional as Frankie's behavior was illegal.

It was just a matter of time before the owners would get rid of Frankie one last time. Rumors were floating around the office that he was getting fired. I started putting together a proposal for the job of Program Director. Hal was asking me to step up and make myself known, and I didn't hesitate. I didn't think I would get the job, but nevertheless, I threw my hat in the ring.

The week after I handed in my proposal, Frankie called a station meeting. Before it started, he said he wanted to see me in his office. I went in, expecting to be briefed on a new promotion, contest or giveaway. Instead, Frankie started barking at me.

"You played the New Edition song at the wrong time," he said, avoiding eye contact as usual. New Edition's reunion album, *Home Again,* had just been released, and we were playing the first single.

"Are you sure?" I asked him. "Maybe the playlist was just mixed up."

"No," Frankie said, raising his voice. "You played the song 20 minutes late!"

"Are you serious?" I asked.

"You're out of here," Frankie said.

I couldn't believe what I was hearing. And then I realized what it was about. "Is this about me applying for the job as Program Director?" I asked.

"Get out of my office!" he yelled.

"Not a problem," I said. "I'm on my way out of *your* office right now. And don't worry, so are you."

Two weeks later, Frankie was fired, and he would never return to WBLS. Pierre Sutton was also fired. Four years later, Frankie would be dead of pancreatic cancer. No one knew Frankie was sick, not even his mother and close friends. He was a man who lived flamboyantly at the center of the in-crowd, but he died alone.

WBLS brought me back to the station after Frankie was terminated. The new General Manager had hired a new Program Director to replace Frankie, and he was wearing a very familiar outfit: a blue suit with a white shirt and a red tie. Yes, to my chagrin, my old nemesis Lee Michaels was back in my life.

Chapter 7: Crossing the Line

Initially, I thought seeing Lee just was a bad dream. Was I imagining things? Lee Michaels? Here at WBLS? The more I thought about it, though, the more it made sense that Kernie Anderson, the new General Manager who had replaced Pierre Sutton, would bring his old colleague on board.

Kernie and Lee had worked together at WBMX in Chicago. I thought Kernie was a nice guy, but as far as I was concerned, his decision to hire Lee Michaels as the Program Director was a formula for the station's failure. I'd learned a lot from my days at Majic. I knew Lee Michaels knew nothing about New York City and that he wouldn't be able to bring anything of value to the table to help WBLS out of its slump. Lee was a pop music guy; he didn't have an ear for the music our listeners wanted to hear.

I'd also learned that it wasn't my job to try to figure out how to save the station. I was not disappointed that I didn't get the job as Program Director. It just never occurred to me that Lee Michaels would get it. Lee started off flashing a few fake smiles and pretending that he and I liked each other. I paid him no mind and continued to commute back and forth to D.C., still working for BET part-time and trying to get more voice-over work.

It was during this time that Nielsen's Broadcast Data Systems (BDS) service began to catch on. The BDS service tracked and monitored the airplay of songs based on the number of spins and detections. Before BDS, Program Directors would write down on paper what they were playing on the radio and submit the information to whoever wanted it. If a disc jockey wrote down that she was playing Marvin Gaye's "Sexual Healing" 20 times per week, music publications like *Billboard* assumed that the station was keeping accurate records.

Of course, that procedure led to corruption. Record companies had been paying for "adds" or additions to radio playlists since the beginning of commercial radio, but how did they know who was really playing the record and how often? They didn't. And many Program Directors would add songs to the playlist, be paid for adding them and never actually play the records. But with the advent of BDS, paper tracking of adds was over. Now, the record labels knew exactly what stations were playing their records and when their records were being played.

BDS would present a bit of a problem for Lee Michaels, who flourished in the old school world of payola-friendly radio. When he came to WBLS, Lee quickly became notorious for adding as many new songs as he could in any given week. I thought Frankie was bad for having us play Maxwell's "Ascension" over and over, but Lee Michaels took record adds to new levels. He was colluding with several independent promoters who brought music and cash to Program Directors in exchange for getting spins for their clients' records.

The rumor around the office was that Lee charged $2,500 to add a song to the playlist. In one week, Lee added 17 records, when no radio station would ever add more than five records in a typical week. I could only imagine how much money he got that week. But it was beginning to catch up with him. The station wasn't playing all the records he was adding, and now with BDS sending out detailed lists, the labels were getting angry. For a while, Lee blamed it on the Nielsen BDS system, claiming that it wasn't properly reporting the songs the station was playing. Eventually, the record labels would start calling up the disc jockeys to get a better sense of what was being played. Lee was slowly being exposed. It didn't seem to matter, though, because he continued to receive valuable perks.

Around the time that Lee Michaels was adding records every week in a frenzy, I got an interesting phone call. I was one of the first customers to have the caller ID feature, and I looked at my display and saw the name Joey Bonner, an old school indie promoter who was known as the best in the business.

I'd known Joey for years. Back when I was working at WKYS, I'd seen him at a convention in Atlantic City. Something had gone wrong with my reservation, and I didn't have a hotel room. Joey Bonner got me a room and told me to think nothing of it. Later that night, I watched him playing Baccarat in the casino. He won $40,000 in 12 minutes. He told me I was good luck, gave me $1,000 and walked out.

I had no idea why Joey Bonner would be calling me now. I answered, and it was Lee Michaels on the phone.

"What's up Lee?" I said.

"Hey, Paul Porter," Lee said. "I wanted to make sure you had my new phone number."

He was living rent-free in a $4,000 a month apartment owned by Joey Bonner. Lee was too stupid to update the phone service, so the number was in Joey's name. To make matters worse, everyone knew that Frankie Crocker had lived in the same apartment when he was at the station. We had a good laugh behind Lee's back. While he was pretending to be the man, living in a fancy spot, we all knew that he was just shacking up in Joey's crib.

Lee had put together a radio promotion for Labor Day weekend. His plan was to play music mixes from his days at WBMX for the entire weekend. Every hour, we would give away $1,075 to the 107th caller. It was a typical promotion, but as usual, Lee had the logistics all wrong. First of all, we weren't actually promoting anything; we were just playing old music. A promotion should be tied to something — it could be as simple as station identification, where you make the winning caller give you the "phrase that pays" in order to get them to listen and pay attention. But there were no parameters to his contest. For the entire weekend, we gave away $60,000 for no good reason.

Here's the worst part: Lee decided to hold the contest during a holiday weekend when most people were away on vacation. So even with the contest running, we had fewer callers than usual. It was pathetic. In fact, it was so unofficial that all of the jocks just gave the money away to people we knew. On my shift, I'd be on the air, pretending to answer the phones and count down to the 107th caller and then — surprise — it would be one of my friends on the line, who actually lived in Boston and couldn't even hear me. I had a friend whose daughter was going off to college and — surprise! — she was a 107th caller too.

Yes, it was unethical. But by then, I was slowly getting sucked into the underbelly of the industry. Frankie was crooked, and Lee was as dirty as they came. Meanwhile, my boy Ricky, a Program Director for an AM station in Hartford, was tracking his payola in a composition notebook. Everyone was getting money and perks. I was working part-time and hustling to get voice-over work. I rationalized that giving away money to people who needed it was not as bad as what everyone else was doing. But of course, it all starts somewhere.

I assumed Lee wouldn't last much longer. He was too dirty and too sloppy, and sure enough, soon after he tried to add 17 new records to the playlist, he was fired. When I heard that Lee was gone, I asked Hal Jackson to consider Vinny Brown for the position. Vinny and I went back to my days in D.C. I thought he was a congenial guy, friendly and cool. He had been out of work for nearly a year when I recommended that Hal call him up. I wanted Vinny to get the job because I thought he was a good fit. I was also hoping that he would look out for me. Lee Michaels had me working overnights, and I knew Vinny would at least be able to get me a better shift.

Vinny did get the job, and I was happy to see him on board. But it didn't take long for me to see the *real* Vinny Brown. He wasn't the same nice guy I knew years before. He was a little *too* full of himself, and it wasn't cool. He came in boasting about the changes he was going to make: Hal Jackson's Sunday show would be cut to halftime, and Champagne, one of the DJs, would be fired.

Although Vinny had a pop radio voice that belonged in a McDonald's commercial, he made himself the voice of the station and redid all of the WBLS promotions using his voice. Fortunately, that ended up being the only major change he made, as Kernie

Anderson blocked Vinny's other ideas. Vinny seemed to quickly grow frustrated and disillusioned.

Vinny did switch me to a better shift on Saturdays, but other jocks didn't fare as well. Raymond Anthony was one of the highest paid jocks on the station. Vinny didn't like Raymond and wanted to fire him, but Raymond was protected by his contract. During Vinny's first week on staff, he screamed at Raymond for something meaningless while Raymond was on the air. This would become a signature Vinny Brown move — calling a jock while they were on the air to curse them out. Raymond was upset, and I thought Vinny's behavior was rude and ridiculous.

It was only a matter of time before Vinny would start in on me, too. During one of my shows, I broadcasted live from Black Expo, a multi-day shopping exhibit at a convention center. During the day, Mike Tyson's manager came over and asked if I'd like to interview the boxer, and I agreed. I interviewed Tyson briefly and got a call from Vinny while I was on the air.

"Yo, motherfucker," he said. "Did I say you could interview Mike Tyson?"

I had spent the entire day talking to old ladies who'd bought ceramic figurines, and here he was cursing me out about a Mike Tyson interview?

"I ain't say interview no motherfucking Mike Tyson!" he screamed. Then he hung up on me. If he would have said that to my face, I might have beaten him down. All I could do was curse him out before he hung up. After that, he didn't schedule me for a shift for two weeks. That was his favorite way to punish jocks: hurt them in the pockets. In New York, missing two shifts on the weekend could mean not having enough money to pay rent.

I'm not sure what had happened to Vinny. I don't know if he started feeling important because he was in New York. He seemed to forget that I knew him when he was struggling to get ahead, using his weak voice on a country music station. But I know it happens all the time — people get a bit of status and forget where they came from.

Vinny Brown stayed at WBLS until it closed down. He became like a member of the Sutton family. Ever since WBLS scored Wendy Williams for the afternoon drive slot, and later, Steve Harvey, Vinny started strutting around with his chest poking out like a peacock. He takes credit for bringing Wendy's popular show to the station, but it was actually General Manager Kernie Anderson who made that happen.

I speculate that one of the reasons why Vinny's personality changed was the way record label reps treated him. Record reps are experts at making Program Directors feel important. I know Vinny took free trips to Brazil and hung out in strip clubs with various record execs. From what I'd heard, Vinny had gone right into Lee Michaels' mode, charging labels — through their independent promoters, of course — up to $2,000 to add a record to the WBLS playlist.

I knew things were getting out of hand in terms of payola when I went to visit an old friend who worked in promotions at Sony. At his office on Madison Avenue, he showed me the contents of his briefcase; it was loaded with cash. I asked him how much. He winked, smiled and told me it was over $10,000. He was on his way to D.C. to take a Vice President at Radio One out to dinner. I knew Vinny had to be getting serious cash, too, but he probably wasn't getting as much money as that VP at Radio One, since Vinny only programmed one station, while Radio One owned several stations across the country.

In my personal life, I'd gone through a rough patch. Since coming to New York, I'd lost my first girlfriend, JoAnn, whom I'd reconnected with when I came back to town. My first boss Sunny Joe White had passed away, and my good friend, musician George Howard, had succumbed to colon cancer when he was only 36 years old. It was a sad time for me. Plus, I'd hit a cold streak with voice-over work. By 1999, the jobs were few and far between. Being in New York with no money was definitely not fun. Vinny was playing games, putting me on the schedule only when he felt like it.

Nevertheless, in my life, whenever one door closes, another always miraculously opens. When I was a young jock in Boston, Donnie Simpson moved me to D.C. for the job of a lifetime. I was devastated when I was fired, but before I could even digest it, I was working for Cathy Hughes at Majic. Then, after she fired me, I was working at BET before I could even get over my anger.

Now, while languishing in New York, working part-time at WBLS and searching for nonexistent voice-over work, another dream job was about to land in my lap. On a Thursday in March of 1999, I got a phone call from Cindy Mahmoud, Vice President of Development at BET. Would I like to come in and work as Program Director? And could I start on Monday? The answers to both questions were a resounding "Yes." In a matter of a few days, I left an erratic part-time position on a poorly rated station to become the Program Director at BET. I'd gone from powerless to powerful. Every urban record label executive in the country would be vying for my attention.

Soon after I accepted the job, I went to a party where Vinny Brown introduced me to music executive Kedar Massenburg.

"Kedar, this is Paul Porter," Vinny said. "He's one of my part-timers."

"Yeah, I'm his part-timer," I said, shaking Kedar's hand. "And I'm also the new Program Director at BET. I look forward to working with you." The look on Vinny's face was priceless.

My job as Program Director came right in the nick of time. I was flat broke. It was getting to the point that I was making the rounds to visit folks at radio stations just so I could get new CDs and sell them for quick cash. I took a Greyhound bus to D.C. for my new job with less than $80 to my name. When I left New York City to catch the bus, my boy Tony Johnson, then the Vice President of Publicity at Mercury/Def Jam Records, met me downstairs at Third and Park Avenue and gave me $200. It felt like a fortune.

I wouldn't be on staff at BET. I was hired as a contracted employee with a salary of $60,000 per year. Cindy Mahmoud had been in a pinch to hire someone quickly. The day before she called me, the previous Program Director, Greg Diggs, had resigned abruptly. I tried reaching out to Greg to find out why he'd left suddenly, but I couldn't get in touch with him. I'd heard that he was having a hard time balancing his spirituality with the video content on the station.

I found out later why Greg Diggs had quit his job. After seeing a video with a few raunchy lines and scenes in it, Greg told Sylvia Rhone she needed to edit some of the content. Sylvia had the video edited and resubmitted it. Greg still wasn't satisfied and asked for more edits. Sylvia said no. She'd already gone way over budget on the video and she expected him to start playing it — immediately. Greg stood his ground. He thought some of the images in the video were inappropriate and said he wasn't playing it without further edits. Sylvia took it up with Bob Johnson, who intervened and told Greg to play the video. Greg quit instead.

I gave Greg Diggs a lot of credit for that. He was the first person I knew to walk out on a good job because of his principles. Greg stood up for standards, while BET didn't. I could respect that, but I couldn't imagine that video content would pose a problem for me. I arrived in D.C. excited about my new job. The bus stopped at Union Station, a short distance from the Hotel George, where BET was putting me up. It was just a block away from the Hyatt, where I'd stayed when Donnie Simpson brought me down from Boston years before.

As soon as I got to BET, I met with Cindy Mahmoud. She told me to take a week to look over the system, meet with the show producers and figure out what the station needed. Cindy made it clear to me right away what she wanted: higher ratings.

"Paul," she told me more than once. "It's your show. Do what you have to do to get the ratings up." She couldn't say it enough. I didn't understand why ratings had suddenly become so important when they had never been important before, but I would soon find out.

On my first day, I went into Greg's computer to see the playlist of videos that were running on the channel. There were more than

1,000 titles in the library, and most of them were crap. BET had always had a reputation for playing anything and everything that was sent to them. It seemed to have gotten way out of hand.

I met with Craig Henry, the producer of "Rap City." During my initial tenure at the station, BET highlighted "Video Soul" with Donnie Simpson. This time around, "Rap City" was BET's most popular show. Shows like "Planet Groove," "Video LP," and "In Your Ear" had failed because BET tried to make cheap shows for a young audience. BET had become a rap music network, and they were down to "Rap City" as their anchor show.

What shocked me the most during that first day on the job was how stuck in the dark ages the station seemed to be. This was 1999, and no one at the company had an email address. Nothing was digitized. The library of songs was written on paper, and staff made manual entries of new videos that were added into rotation. I was shocked by the inefficiency.

BET did have the Selector software to schedule music, but they weren't using it properly. Some shows had dead air because the time entered for the videos was incorrect. Some producers were scrambling to fill minutes of empty space when their shows didn't fill the time allotted. And anyone who has ever watched BET knows the frustration of watching one show end with a certain video just to see the next show begin with the same video.

I knew I had a lot of work to do. I had to find a crew within the staff that I could trust, come up with a game plan and execute it. I had inherited Greg Diggs' assistant, and I wasn't happy with her. She was a sweet-acting woman who had worked at BET for so many years that we called her a "lifer." It quickly became clear to me that industry executives had buttered her up for years in order to gain access to Greg, and she was trying to keep those contacts. It was funny. She was a deeply religious woman who listened only to gospel music and didn't like the videos shown on BET. Yet she'd developed relationships with record labels to make sure those videos she detested got played. In exchange, they hooked her up with gospel CDs and tickets to gospel plays.

Those first few days, she was watching my every move to see if I was going to do things the way Greg did them. And she was constantly telling me how to do my job. I didn't confide in her. Just because I had inherited Greg's assistant didn't mean I was going to inherit Greg's way of doing business. Instead, I focused on the young people on staff. Two people stood out to me: Tuma Basa, who worked in the programming department, and Chezik Walker, who was a young producer. They were both talented and hardworking. I remember Tuma putting together a PowerPoint presentation for my first staff meeting. I could see that the other staff members were "hating on him" because he did a great job. Tuma didn't care what the so-called cool kids thought. I knew he would be good for my team. I made Tuma my new assistant, and Chezik became an unofficial member of my team.

Over the next week, we watched hundreds of videos. I couldn't make heads or tails of how most of the titles had been entered into the Selector software. I sent the hard drive to the DJ who had taught me the program. He said it was a waste of money for BET to have purchased the software if they were going to use it so ineffectively.

I wasn't ready to talk to anybody in the music industry yet, but the calls started coming in fast and furious. The week before, I had been walking the streets of New York, broke. Now, I was telling Tuma to let the record reps know that I would have to call them back.

Soon it would begin for me. Just like Frankie Crocker, Lee Michaels, Vinny Brown and countless others who had been lured in before me, I would start to believe my own hype and get sucked into everything I felt was wrong with the urban music industry. My boy Ricky from WBLS called, and I *did* speak to him. He congratulated me and told me I was going to get paid. He told me that the numbers I'd seen in his composition book were nothing compared to the money I would be offered to get videos on the air.

I knew that I was in a position that could come with payola perks, but I didn't know much about how that worked. I was just happy to have a job. I wasn't about to tell a record rep that they had to pay me to get a video in rotation. I listened to my boy Ricky, but I didn't put much stock into what he was saying. I did know that I was suddenly very popular with all my old industry folks and even some I didn't know. My second day at BET, I got a call from a rep working for a popular urban record label.

"Hey Paul!" she said, as if we were old friends. "What size shirt do you wear?"

I had never met the lady, and she wanted to know my shirt size. The next day, I had a black jacket with my name stitched in it. The day after that, it was a box of designer label clothes with all the newest shirts, pants, and coats. Every label was sending boxes of CDs. I got at least 500 CDs in the first week.

After watching a mind-numbing number of videos, I decided I was going to cut 500 of them out of the library right away. If it was outdated, poorly shot, or just plain corny, the video was gone. I talked to everyone at the station, from camera operators to talent like Tigger, Joe Clair, and Big Lez, who were hosting "Rap City," and Rachel, who was hosting "Planet Groove." Most of the shows were just running videos, some even without a host or without voice-overs.

BET was on the air 24 hours a day, but I knew that most viewers watched in the evening, after school and after work, so I decided to focus on the hours of 4 to 8 p.m. and beef up the playlist. At the time, BET didn't play anything in heavy rotation; there were so many videos in rotation that even the most popular videos were airing, at most, only 13 or 15 times a week. I planned to shape the playlist as I did when I took over as Program Director for Cathy Hughes at Majic: I was going to shrink the library, play the hits and cut out the duds.

I knew drastic changes to the playlist were going to shock the urban music industry, but it had to be done. I was prepared to take the risk. I avoided talking to any label reps while I was deciding which songs would be put into heavy rotation, which songs wouldn't and which ones would be cut altogether.

Before I could finalize the playlist, I had other fires to put out. BET was the redheaded stepchild of the music video industry. It aired in 66 million households, while MTV was in 100 million households. Nevertheless, BET was responsible for launching a lot of careers. It was the only video outlet that focused on black artists, and it was important. Up until that point, the station was considered a steppingstone to get to MTV. But BET actually had a strong hand, and I was going to use it. I was determined to get the station some respect.

As I was planning the playlist, I looked up Sean "Puffy" Combs' song with Nas, "Hate Me Now," to see how often it was in rotation. I couldn't find it anywhere in the computer, and then I was informed that I couldn't find it because we didn't have it. Puffy had given MTV an exclusive, and BET wouldn't be able to play the video for another month. I called up Jeff at Bad Boy.

"There's nothing we can do," he said. "We've got a contract with MTV."

"Give your boy Puff a message," I said. "If he's going to give exclusives to MTV, we will be exclusively not playing any videos by any of his artists."

I was brash, cocky and making up my own rules as I went along. I didn't feel beholden to anyone. Of course, my personality occasionally clashed with some of the artists who were featured on the channel. I was doing things differently, and not everyone was cool with it.

I met with producers of "Rap City," who told me about being turned down by Master P, rapper and founder of No Limit Records, for an interview on location at an awards show. Master P told them he didn't have time because he had to do an interview with MTV. I knew Master P's history with BET — the station had practically made him. I asked my assistant to get his people on the phone, and I talked to Shelly at Profile Records. I told her about what had happened at the awards show and that we'd be boycotting Master P in protest. She said, "You can't do that!" I said, "Watch me." I pulled his videos off the station.

A few weeks after I'd initiated the Master P blackout, I received a phone call: The voice had a New Orleans drawl.

"This is P. Why you ain't playing my shit?" he said.

I told him until he gave BET respect, I was not playing anything by him or his artists.

The next day, Master P came to my office. He was into wrestling, and he brought some wrestlers with him. He opened my office door, and I pulled out my Smith & Wesson 9 millimeter gun.

"Hey man, sit down," I said. "We're not going to have any Steve Stoute and Puffy-type trouble in here, are we?" I asked Master P, referring to the champagne bottle beat-down Puffy had given out the week before.

His assistant said to me, "Man, you are crazy?"

I said, "You can't diss BET and go to MTV if this is where your bread is made."

He looked at me as if he were sizing me up. "I like this nigga," he said with his flashy smile.

We sat down to watch the video he'd brought, "Souljahs." It was an animated video, and Master P went on and on about how it cost $1 million to make and how it was going to make history. I had never seen such a horrible video in my life. It was a low-budget cartoon with toy army men that came to life and started rapping.

As awful as his video was, I put it into rotation, but there wasn't enough money printed in the world that would make me play that corny video more than five times per week. We only played the video for two weeks before we dropped it from the playlist entirely. I put Master P's other videos back on, and we became friendly.

I knew I had power, but I didn't know how crazy it could get until I got a call from Dorsey James, the President of LaFace Records. He wanted to make sure I was going to play the video for Donell Jones' "Say What." I already knew of and liked the song; we'd played it on WBLS. I knew I was going to play the video, and I told him not to worry about it.

But Dorsey wasn't taking any chances. He told me that he was about to hire someone to work in video promotion, and he'd narrowed it down to two candidates. He wanted me to choose who should get the job. I was puzzled. Why the hell would I choose who got the job? I didn't work for the record company.

"Since you'll be working closely with whoever we hire, it's important that it's someone you'll be able to get along with," he told me. I thought that was just crazy. They were basically asking me choose the person so that I would be invested; they figured if I chose the candidate, I'd take the calls, play the videos and in general have a favorable relationship with the label. I ended up choosing Chanel Green, who worked for Jive. She was a single mother, and I've always had a weakness for kids.

JC Ricks, the National Promotions Director for LaFace, told me that Dorsey wanted to send me a present, and asked me what I needed. I thought about what my boy Ricky from WBLS said about getting paid. Were they asking me if I wanted cash? I wasn't sure, and I wasn't trying to find out. I told him I needed a cell phone. When Dorsey, JC, and I went out to lunch the next day, they brought me a Motorola flip phone that had just come on the market. Over lunch, as they continued to beat me over the head about the Donell Jones video, they offered me more perks, like trips to exotic locations. I listened and nodded. It all sounded good. I opened the phone up at the end of the lunch, but it wasn't activated. JC told me to just send him the bill after I got the phone turned on.

I knew it wasn't legal to get a free cell phone or a leather jacket, but I assumed those were the perks of being a Program Director for a major station. It didn't seem like a big deal to me. I knew there were people at BET who were getting much more than a free cell phone.

After three weeks, I was ready to send out my first playlist. I emailed it — a first at the station — and waited for the yells and screams. If a label had five videos, I ended up cutting about three of them. The two remaining videos went from three spins a week to 15 spins a week. That created a problem. In my meetings, I'd tried to explain: My plan was to play new videos a lot, during the early life of the album, when labels were pushing for sales. On the back end, I was taking the videos off as they climbed up the chart to make room for the next soon-to-be hits. I had no intention of continually playing the videos until viewers got sick of them. I loved Q-Tip's "Vivrant Thing," and it went from zero spins to being the Number 1 video on the network. Record reps were pissed off! I didn't care. Sometimes, you have to take drastic measures to create change. I wasn't backing off, not even when it came to the artists who'd enjoy carte blanche at the station for years.

One of the few people who appreciated the new order of business was Kevin Liles at Def Jam. His artists, including Ja Rule, got lots of airplay around the time of their album release, which led to strong first week sales. Things were working the way they were supposed to work. I had the acts playing in heavy rotation on the station and, in turn, the labels were getting decent sales.

In order for this to work well for the labels, the acts had to be hot. Arista Records was struggling with superstar diva acts like Toni Braxton and Whitney Houston. One of the first people I had to battle with was Lionel Ridenour at Arista Records. The last time I saw him, we'd driven to a mutual friend's wedding together. I was cool with Lionel, but I'd heard that, like Vinny Brown, he turned into a yeller and a screamer when he got into a position of power.

Lionel was working Whitney Houston's latest album, *My Love Is Your Love*. The title single was awful, and the video was worse. I had the video on my new playlist 12 times a week, which was a lot for that song. But Lionel was pissed because it wasn't getting the 28 spins per week that "Vivrant Thing" was getting. He called me up to complain, and I tried to explain my new formula. He wasn't trying to hear it.

"You're playing Donell Jones 20 times a week!" he yelled.

I had to look at the phone and shake my head. "Donnell Jones is your artist too!" I said. I didn't know that executives like Lionel were being instructed to push harder for Arista artists as opposed to those distributed by Arista for LaFace.

"Look man," I said to Lionel. "What do you want me to do? You want me to flip Donell's number of spins with Whitney's?"

I knew he'd never go for that. In all honesty, I was just being cocky.

"No," Lionel said. "I want you to flip Q-Tip's spins for Whitney's. She's an icon." Lionel hung up on me.

Yeah, I thought to myself, *she's an icon, but that song sucks.*

Four days later, my assistant told me that Cindy Mahmoud wanted to see me in her office. Cindy's office was a long walk away from mine, so I knew it couldn't be good news. Lionel Ridenour had written a memo to Bob Johnson and sent a copy to Cindy. It was a strongly worded memo about a "serious problem" with airtime for one of Arista's biggest acts, Whitney Houston, and how she was not getting the support she should from a label that supported BET. Lionel was going hard, implying that Arista would pull ads if BET didn't play Whitney's videos. Cindy told me not to worry about it. She said it was bad that he'd sent the memo directly to Bob Johnson, but that Bob had obviously received it and not responded. No news from him meant he wasn't getting involved. Cindy told me to keep it moving and not give it another thought.

In typical Paul Porter style, I couldn't just let it go. I wrote my response memo backed up with lots of research on Whitney's record. The first week sales had been terrible. Her labelmate, newcomer Donell Jones, was playing on more radio stations than she was. And Q-Tip had sold three times as many albums in the same time period. According to my new formula for spins, Whitney's video should have only been played *six* times per week. I was playing it twice as much.

I addressed my memo to Clive Davis and copied Lionel on it.

"Why did you send that memo to my boss?" Lionel asked me.

"At least I sent it to you, too," I said. "I didn't even know about your letter until someone showed it to me."

"You know what?" Lionel said. "You need to talk to my man."

"What man? Who is he?" I asked.

"He handles my problems," Lionel responded.

I didn't know what Lionel was talking about. Was he going to send someone to beat me up?

"Do you have a cell phone?" he asked. *Yeah*, I thought to myself. *Your company is paying the bill.* I gave him the number and he told me to expect a call.

As soon as I hung up with Lionel, I called my boy Ricky and asked him if he knew the man. He started laughing. "He's the best," he told me. "Now you're about to see what I'm talking about."

Sure enough, I received a call on my cell. "I'm trying to get some more spins for Arista," he said. "Where are you staying?"

I gave him my address at the Hotel George. "You'll get a package from me on Saturday morning," he said before hanging up.

As soon as I heard the words "Saturday morning," I had a flashback. At WBLS, I used to talk to a guy who knew everyone's business. He'd told me something about Lee Michaels always getting cash from indie promoters who worked for the record labels, and it always came on Saturday mornings in a FedEx package.

All of the trips, the meals, the clothes, and the phone I had gotten were nothing. What I thought was payola was just year-round holiday gift giving. I had no idea how deep payola could get. But I knew I was about to find out.

That Saturday morning, I called the front desk first thing and told the woman there I was expecting a package and asked her to look out for it. She called me later that morning and told me the package had arrived. I ran downstairs at the speed of light and rushed back to my suite. The return label said "Karen Kline, Miami, Florida." There was no street address. I opened it up and saw two packs of $100 bills wrapped in plastic. I counted $5,000 in each pack. There was no note. Sunny Joe and Donnie Simpson did not bring me into the game to go dirty like this. But I was fed up with being broke. By that point I had two sons to take care of; one was in college with tuition bills.

I had watched Lee Michaels scam his way from station to station, getting fired every few years but still getting paid. I thought about getting fired from Majic and getting a week's worth of severance pay. Now, I was at the top of the food chain, and I knew BET could be my last stop.

I decided I wasn't going to take money from just anybody. But I wasn't sending the money back to Karen Kline either. I also knew I still wasn't playing Whitney's video. I wasn't sure if there was a way I could take money from a select few to maintain relationships and still have some integrity in my programming choices. I put the money in my safe and decided I was going to try to find out.

The weekend after I received my first package from Karen Kline, I received another FedEx package that contained $5,000 in cash. It included a letter telling me which record label the payment was from. The payments were not for particular songs; they were sent to maintain a relationship. The labels weren't telling me what to play. They just wanted me to be happy. I took the money and developed the playlist the way I wanted it.

Payola extended far beyond the packages from Karen Kline. Every weekend, I traveled back to New York for my weekend shift at WBLS, and I would hit up a different record label to pay my expenses — Jive, VP Records, Interscope, MCA, Motown, Def Jam. I never paid my own airfare or hotel costs. And I always insisted on staying at the Hotel Benjamin or the W Hotel, where rates could go for more than $500 per night.

The well-known indie promoters had a discreet operation going, and I felt safe. They knew what they were doing, and I knew I wouldn't get in trouble for it. Some of the smaller labels and independent promoters were not as polished. One weekend, I was at a hotel in New York going through packages of videos that people had sent in. I got one from a New York DJ and his partner, who worked at Epic Records. They were trying to get a record deal for an act they'd discovered. I thought the guy sounded too much like The Notorious B.I.G., and I wasn't interested. But they were still on the grind, trying desperately to get the video on BET. I thought they were hustling backwards. They didn't have a record deal, and the rapper didn't have any radio airplay. But they were trying to get the video on BET so that they could sell wolf tickets to the labels and get a deal. Without opening the package, I gave it to a friend. When he got home, he called me and said there was $1,000 stuffed inside the package. I told him he needed to get back to my hotel room.

I couldn't believe that people were taking those kinds of risks. They didn't even tell me ahead of time that I was getting cash through the mail, like it was nothing. That's when I realized how pervasive payola had become. You didn't even need to meet with someone face-to-face. You just stuffed some cash in an envelope with the video and hoped for the best. I received a call to find out if I'd gotten the package. I used the fact that I wasn't expecting it as an excuse and told him I never got it. I never played the video, but I kept the money. It was official. I was on the take. I wasn't nearly as outlandish as I could have been, but it was enough to make me dirty.

Messing around with some of the low-level promoters got annoying. Willie Young, a D.C.-area producer and host of a local video show, was a prime example. All of the staffers of "Rap City" were flying down to Myrtle Beach for a "Ruff Ryders Weekend" sponsored by Ducati, the motorcycle manufacturer. Willie asked me if I'd like to host a show he was promoting in Myrtle Beach that weekend for R&B group Jagged Edge. He offered to pay me $1,000, and I accepted. I was going to be there anyway with the staff of "Rap City," and an extra thousand dollars wouldn't hurt.

But the show was cancelled because no one showed up, and although Willie had paid me $500 when I first arrived, after the show was cancelled, he was nowhere to be found with the other half of my money. I was determined to get my $500, and I ended up using just the *idea* of payola to get my money back. After I returned from Myrtle Beach, I finally heard from Willie, who apologized for skipping out on me. He then asked me for a favor. He was trying to get a local act from Miami onto BET, and they had $2,000 to spend to get the video on the air. I knew Willie's game. He would use his relationships with people like me to con local acts. He'd tell them they needed $3,000 to get a video on BET, then he'd tell me the group had $2,000 and keep $1,000 for himself.

I knew Willie was trying to make some money for himself, too, even though he was pretending like he was just trying to help the group. I didn't care either way. I knew the group was probably not good enough to get onto my playlist, and I knew all I wanted from Willie Young was my $500.

I agreed to play the video for $2,000. Willie Young flew up the very next day and came to my office at BET to give me the money. I took out $500 and gave the rest of the money back to him.

"What are you doing?" he asked.

"I just wanted my money back," I told him. "You can get out now."

"Come on, Paul," he pleaded. "That's not right."

"You should have paid me in Myrtle Beach," I said. "I had to do what I had to do to get my money back." Willie left the video with me, and as I expected, it was garbage. I never played it.

Record companies had some slick ways of getting around payola, either by using indie promoters as middle men or finding creative ways to pay me directly.

Soon after I returned from Myrtle Beach, I spoke to Kevin Liles, then president of Def Jam. He asked me if I enjoyed the weekend, and I told him I did and said I fell in love with one of the Ducati bikes. Kevin offered me a side job recording a voice-over for a commercial for one of his new artists, an R&B singer named Case. The commercial would only air on one station in New York, and it would only take me a few minutes to record it. I agreed to do it, although I knew it would only make me a few hundred dollars. I recorded the commercial, and then I called Kevin's office to find out the amount I should put on the invoice I was sending to the company. The receptionist put me on hold and then came back on the line. She told me to put down $8,000. I sent in the invoice and got a check a week later. I was obviously being paid for a lot more than just the 10 minutes of work I put into recording that commercial.

Within a year, I'd made at least $40,000 in extra cash from indie promoters acting at the behest of major record labels and from executives who funneled cash to me other ways. Adding up the cost of travel expenses that many labels paid for would also tally into the thousands. But the cash wouldn't keep flowing for long. Those things never continue indefinitely. And after less than a year at BET, big changes were on the way.

Five months after I started at BET, Cindy Mahmoud called me into her office to let me know that Debra Lee, BET's Chief Operating Officer, was replacing her with someone new. Cindy wasn't being fired, just transferred to a post she'd held before, Vice President of Creative Services. Cindy was not happy about the decision, and she was making plans to leave the company. She told me her replacement was going to be Stephen Hill, a D.C. native who was working in MTV's programming department. I knew of Stephen Hill, but didn't know him well. I used to see him in D.C. at various concerts, and I knew he'd started his radio career at my old station, WILD in Boston. Everything I heard about him centered around the fact that he was a crossover guy; he liked rock music and was generally known as the black guy at MTV.

During the first meeting I had with Stephen, he didn't look me in the eye. I took that as a bad sign. He sat down with me and looked at the playlist and just nodded his head. He told me he liked all of the changes and that he wanted to have a meeting with me the next week before I added any new videos. Cindy Mahmoud had never asked to see the playlist. As Vice President, she concentrated on developing shows and extending the life of the brand, so I was surprised when Stephen said he wanted to be more hands-on with the videos I selected. He was supposed to be creating new programs, putting out fires, dealing with scheduling issues and talent, and determining BET's future. But it seemed like he was immediately more concerned with the music than the actual network.

The following week, I met with Stephen, who was spitting out questions left and right. Why was I adding this video? Why wasn't I adding that video? He told me that MTV followed the charts and only added videos with at least 2,500 spins at urban radio. Stephen Hill was a numbers man, a nod I suppose to his degree in math. He wasn't the type to add a video because it was good. He wanted an external reason for playing a video.

I didn't agree with his methods. First of all, I knew a lot of radio stations were playing songs simply because there was a video out, not because the song was popular. I followed my gut instincts and I looked at sales. If consumers were actually buying a record, I thought that was a better indicator of which videos should be played. On this and many other issues, Stephen Hill and I just couldn't agree. Eventually, I'd walk down the halls of BET and Stephen would make sure to make moves in the opposite direction. If he couldn't get away in time, he'd keep his head down. I noticed that he talked mainly to the younger people on the staff. It seemed obvious that he wanted someone younger in my position, a protégé who would look up to him.

I just waited for the inevitable. Eventually, he called me in for what turned out to be a 30-second meeting. I walked into his office and, as usual, he didn't look me in the eye. He looked extremely nervous, like he thought I would beat him up if he said the wrong thing.

"I think I'm going to be going in a different direction," he said.

"What direction?" I asked.

"I'm going to bring in someone else to do the music, someone younger," he said.

"Just let me know when," I said.

The meeting was over. Although I remained at BET for months, I never spoke to Stephen Hill again. Somehow, he managed to never come within 10 feet of me. He went from the front entrance directly into his office and stayed there, making sure he didn't run into me. He hadn't fired me, so I continued programming the videos. He didn't ask any more questions about the videos I was adding or sit in on any meetings. I heard through friends in the industry that he was interviewing people for the job, so I knew my days were numbered.

At that point, I developed an "F-you" mentality. When I knew I was on my way out, I added four or five videos that I normally wouldn't have added in order to make sure I had some cash before I left. Previously, I'd turned down money from an NBA player's record label, but before I left, I took the $1,500 and added the video. Then Chris Webber had a video to go along with his failed attempt at becoming a rapper, so I scooped up a quick $2,500 and put that on the air as well.

Stephen Hill never actually fired me. I'd heard he was bringing people in on the weekends to show them the ropes. A friend in the legal department warned me that my time was up. I found out that Kelly G, the man chosen by Stephen Hill to replace me, was staying in my hotel. I introduced myself and ended up taking him out to lunch a few times. Kelly seemed like a cool guy, straightforward and direct. I didn't really understand his fashion style. He reminded me of Bernie Mac — print shirts, white pants and a shiny face — but I didn't have any beef with him. I told him straight up that Stephen was out for himself and that he should be, too. He seemed to appreciate the words of wisdom, but I knew what was in store for him, and I was right. Kelly G was known for not having any control over what played on BET. Before he did anything, he had to check with Stephen Hill. Stephen knew that wasn't going to work with me.

In all honesty, I was basically fired from BET by the staff at the Hotel George. I'd stayed at the hotel for the entire year that I worked at BET. My driver's license even listed the hotel as my permanent address. My bill was over $25,000. One morning, the hotel manager called me up and told me that BET was only paying for my stay through the end of the week. I never received anything in writing or even a phone call. I was evicted. And that was how I knew my time at BET was over.

I didn't know it then, but Bob Johnson was already in discussions with Viacom to sell BET. I believe that's why Cindy

Mahmoud was moved aside in favor of someone from MTV who could turn the brand into its urban counterpart. It was all about making the station palatable — bringing up the ratings and polishing up the brand to make it a black version of MTV. And Stephen Hill did exactly that. It was like that scene from the movie *Coming to America* when John Amos' character, who owns a McDowell's restaurant, explains how he copied McDonald's and changed it up a bit to avoid being sued. MTV had a wacky man-on-the-street show called "The Tom Green Show," so Stephen Hill created "Hits From The Street." MTV had "Cribs," so Stephen Hill created "How I'm Livin'." MTV had an afternoon countdown show with "TRL," so Stephen Hill created "106 & Park."

I stayed in the hotel for an extra two weeks, trying to figure out what I was going to do with my life. I'd spent the last year picking out videos for a music channel. I knew I'd done a good job at it, but it seemed like a no-win situation. I was continually bumping heads with people, and I couldn't manage to just suck it up, toe the corporate line and keep a job like everyone else.

I had a little money in the bank, but I had nowhere to go and no job prospects. Back in Boston, when Steve Crumbley fired me from WILD, I went back to the building the next week, hoping to run into some of my industry buddies who could help me out. By this time, I knew better. I knew that whatever industry connections I had would dry up the moment I checked out of the hotel. BET had gotten exactly what they needed from me. I came in and cleaned up the place after Greg Diggs left unexpectedly. Then, when they were ready for some new blood, I was discarded. None of the promotions people at the labels would be paying for my travel anywhere. No more packages from Karen Kline, and no more rent-free living. My power was gone, and so was the payola. It was time for me to find another job.

Chapter 8: The Era of the Shock Jock

After an unsuccessful job hunt in New York City, I returned to D.C. and rented an apartment on Capitol Hill. In a matter of days, I heard from Cindy Mahmoud. She'd left BET soon after Stephen Hill arrived, and she was now working at a startup station called New Urban Entertainment Television (NUE-TV) that was trying to position itself as a family-oriented alternative to BET.

Cindy wanted me to do music programming and help build a music library for the station so they could show vintage videos as well as new releases. I would need to use my contacts to get the library stocked. While Cindy waited to get her budget approved so that I could begin working, I started dabbling in the music industry, doing consulting for independent acts that were trying to get their videos into rotation. I was now playing on the other side of the fence, taking money from artists and telling them I couldn't guarantee anything but I'd make sure their videos got into the right hands.

I started traveling to Miami to visit an old girlfriend, and soon, I was investing money into a music group that had what I felt was good material. I had become another struggling black man with no job, throwing money into a music group, thinking the big payday was just around the corner. I *knew* better. I knew what it really took to get a song on radio or TV. But for a while, I was sucked in, just like any other gambler, thinking that I could make a quick dollar by bringing good music to the masses.

While I was hustling back and forth to Miami, Cindy Mahmoud called. Her budget was approved, and I was hired as the Music Consultant for NUE-TV. I started making calls, asking labels to send their new and old videos. It was easy to get the new releases, but I couldn't get anyone to go into their archives and send me vintage tapes for the library. My boy Dwayne McClary sent down nearly 100 MCA videos, but that was it. Every video rep said the same thing: It wasn't in their budgets to send anything but current videos. It costs money to press up older videos and send them out, and labels weren't about to do that for a start-up station that wasn't even on the air. At that point, the only place you could watch NUE-TV was in its own offices. Labels said that once NUE-TV was airing nationally, they'd be happy to send their old videos.

We all had new Nextel phones, and NUE-TV was paying the bills. I was being paid a decent salary — $60,000 — for a job that involved little more than making phone calls. Cindy even told me I could work from home whenever I wanted. That meant that I was often "working" from Miami Beach. I knew from the start that NUE-TV wasn't going to make it.

They paid radio personality Tom Joyner $500,000 for the rights to film his wedding. I was shocked that any television executive would green light such a stupid move. First of all, who wanted to watch Tom Joyner's wedding? And second of all, why on God's green earth would they spend half a million dollars on any show while the network didn't have any homes to air it in? Those fools even paid for Tom's actual wedding.

The station was airing solely in our office building for the first four months; then, they picked up one digital cable channel in Atlanta. Tom Joyner's wedding was on repeatedly. I read that the station had 2 million subscribers, but I don't know where they got those inflated numbers.

Then there was the whole farce of pretending that NUE-TV was "Quincy Jones' station." All of the media reports talked about how it was his station and he was an investor, and we were encouraged to hype this up; the only problem was, it wasn't true. As far as I knew, Quincy Jones hadn't put up one dollar of his own money. He'd allowed the NUE-TV folks to bounce his name around, but they had to give him a piece of the company for that.

It seemed that NUE-TV execs were trying to employ the "fake it till you make it" strategy. But they just weren't making it. The first real sign that NUE-TV was a sinking ship came when they moved everyone who worked on the business side on the second floor and squeezed them in with the creative people on the first floor. A few weeks later, I was at a local record store in D.C., talking to the owner about stocking a record by one of my artists, when I got a call on my Nextel from one of the staffers. She told me that I should come to the office immediately. I did, just in time to see all of the office furniture and computers being repossessed.

I sat outside with the rest of my co-workers and wondered out loud if life at BET had really been so bad. We all laughed. But it was sad to see a good idea run into the ground. Even if NUE-TV had had better direction, Bob Johnson wasn't going to let it succeed. He'd recently sold part of his company to Comcast, and it's widely believed that Comcast didn't pick up NUE-TV because they were in business with Bob Johnson and BET. Later, I found out that an expected major investment from Radio One (Cathy Hughes' company) never materialized. In addition, a deal with AOL Time Warner never came through.

All of the company cell phones got cut off. Then, the checks started to come in later and later. My boy Tommy worked near Cindy's office. One day, Tommy heard Cindy screaming into the phone that she had a mortgage to pay and that she needed her check.

"When a Vice President starts screaming about getting paid," Tommy said, "you *know* we're in trouble."

Tommy was right. The next day, our checks did not arrive. I stayed in Miami, waiting for word on what was going on. Poor Cindy. Even after we all realized NUE-TV was done, she was still calling me, telling me they were trying to get another round of financing. When it was all over, the company owed me $5,000. It took me two months to get it. I couldn't even be mad at NUE-TV. I'd made enough to live on for a year, and I'd probably made 10 phone calls.

Before long, I was wondering — once again — what my next move should be. It's difficult for a black jock to age gracefully in radio. In pop radio, there are plenty of formats to switch over to, but in Black radio, it's either hip hop or oldies. You're either down with the youth culture or you're playing oldies for the AARP crowd. I wasn't sure where my place was anymore. The radio and television industries that I'd worked in for over 20 years had changed drastically. I was different, too. I'd gone from being naive and innocent to being cutthroat and jive-slick. I wasn't proud of the transformation, but I knew I couldn't go back in time and change the things I'd done. Fortunately, I was about to be given the opportunity to redeem myself.

I returned to New York to see if I could reclaim a job that Toya Beasley at KISS-FM had offered me the year before that I had turned down. I called her, and she offered to put me on the air on weekends and as a fill-in when necessary.

As an urban adult contemporary station, KISS-FM was pretty low-key, with a playlist tame enough for office workers and suburban carpoolers. In fact, the format and the playlist were so tame that I was bored out of my mind. I was playing the same songs I'd programmed at Majic back in 1988.

Radio had lost all the joy and excitement for me. The format had become too stringent. I couldn't talk during the music intros or deviate from what was written on the liner cards. There was no room for spontaneity or creativity. All I could do during music breaks was say the name of the station, say my name and announce the three songs coming up next and introduce each song. How many times can you say, *And now here is Earth, Wind & Fire with "Reasons"?*

From where I sat in the booth at KISS-FM, I could look directly across the hall and see what was going on at their sister station, HOT 97, which had been targeting young people with a steady stream of hardcore hip hop since the early '90s. New York City was one of the biggest markets in radio, so HOT 97 was a nationally recognized brand. No other station worked harder than HOT 97 to immortalize rap music, and no station worked harder than HOT 97 to market vile gangsta rap to black inner-city children. HOT 97 was the national leader for hip hop, and for breaking all the rules.

I worked at KISS-FM, but I felt myself drawn to what was happening at HOT 97. Although I'd said hello (and goodbye) to age 40, I was still in tune with the hip-hop generation and considered myself, if not a full-fledged member, an elder brother of sorts. I was cool with Fatman Scoop and some of the other DJs at the station. We had a lot of bull sessions at the studio, talking about music and politics. I didn't like a lot of what was going on at HOT 97, and I wasn't afraid to express my opinion.

Shock jocks Star (Troi Torain) and his sidekick Buc Wild (Timothy Joseph) had recently been taken off of HOT 97. The "Star & Buc Wild Morning Show" was HOT 97's top-rated show for three years straight. Star and Buc Wild played hip hop and filled the air with racial slurs, misogynistic insults, and insensitive jokes about welfare mothers, Caribbean immigrants, and Black people who supported reparations for slavery. Star was known for lambasting the station's advertisers on air, and he disgracefully played screams on air after the singer Aaliyah died in a plane crash. He had been suspended from the station more times than I can count, but he was always called back in to work.

Star was seeking a new annual contract with HOT 97 worth more than $2.5 million when Barry Mayo came on board to oversee the company's three stations as Senior Vice President for Emmis New York. There was already a heated competition for the hip-hop market between Emmis and Clear Channel Communications, the nation's largest radio operator. Right away, Barry and Star's personalities clashed. When the "Star & Buc Wild Morning Show" fell from third overall to fifth in the Arbitron ratings, Star was taken off the air — this time for good. When Star left HOT 97, he claimed that he ripped 20 award plaques off the station's walls. He also claimed that Barry Mayo withheld two $30,000 checks that were owed to him.

In 2003, HOT 97 hired a new host for the morning drive: Sway (Calloway), an MTV personality and hip-hop artist. Sway had been in a rap group, Sway & Tech. I'd played their video when I was at BET. When I first saw him at the station, he was excited to see me.

"You're the Captain," he said, calling me by the name Donnie Simpson had christened me with years ago. "You played my video on BET!"

Sway and I had a nice talk. With a head full of dreadlocks and a "peace, brother" demeanor, he seemed to be progressive and conscious. Eventually, I found out it was all a facade. When I tried to get airtime on the radio for someone who really deserved it, Sway believed that listeners were not interested.

Aaron Patterson of Chicago had been incarcerated for 17 years and on Death Row for 13 years for two murders that he maintained he did not commit. On his last day in office, the Governor of Illinois pardoned Aaron. After years of protests and a new investigation, Patterson was finally freed and exonerated. One of the most compelling parts of the story was that during the interrogation, Aaron had managed to scratch out a message on a table with a paper clip. "Aaron 4/30 I lied about murders. Police threaten me with violence. Slapped and suffocated me with plastic. No lawyer or dad. No phone. Sign false statement to murders."

I was impressed by his story and by his attempts to help others when he was released from prison. Three days after he was released, he appeared on "The Oprah Winfrey Show" and began traveling and talking to various groups about police brutality. He was given $180,000 in restitution by the city of Chicago, but before he received the check, he took out a loan for $100,000 to bail out another man in prison.

Aaron Patterson came to New York and an old friend of mine, Lisa Fager, asked me to drive him around as he attended a few meetings and spoke to some Civil Rights groups. I met Aaron, and we talked as I helped him make his way around New York. Aaron had been in prison for 17 years, so everything was new to him: technology, politics, and music. It was as if he'd been in a time warp. It was an education for me, because I was able to see our society through the eyes of someone who hadn't seen the gradual changes over the years.

Aaron was shocked and disgusted by what he heard on the radio. In prison, he'd spent more time reading than listening to music, and because he was in solitary confinement most of the time, he didn't come into contact with some of the young people who were coming in off the street. Aaron couldn't believe what hip-hop artists were able to say on the radio. He marveled at the fact that they were essentially spelling out how to make and sell drugs in plain language that anyone could understand. No one questioned it. Aaron also noticed that treatment toward women had changed a lot since he was thrown in jail in 1986.

"I don't understand," he said to me more than once. "Why are they playing this kind of stuff on the radio? This is poison!"

Aaron was saying everything I had been coming to realize. But it sounded even more powerful coming from him, because he had been locked away for so long.

I felt that Aaron had an incredible story to tell, and I decided to help him get on the radio in New York. Black radio used to tell stories like Aaron's, but as I called around to radio DJs, I saw that those times had come and gone. James Mtume, who I'd interviewed on "Fresh" back in the '80s, had a show with Bob Slade called "Open Line." I put in a call there to get Aaron on their show, but because of a personal beef that Bob had with me, they didn't bring him on.

I called Wendy Williams, who was now doing big things with an afternoon drive talk show on WBLS. I told her about Aaron's story and that he'd just been on "The Oprah Winfrey Show" the week before. Wendy agreed that his story should be heard and told me to bring him up the station the next day at 4 p.m.

The next day, Aaron and I went to WBLS and waited in the lobby. After a while, Wendy's producer came out to tell us that she was going to have to cancel. Wendy and I went too far back for her to send a producer out to cancel on me after talking to me personally about having Aaron on the show. I was angry, and Aaron even more so. I went back to the studio and asked Wendy what the problem was. She told me she thought Aaron's story was too serious for her audience. I knew that Wendy's audience could handle a brief segment on Aaron, and I believe she knew it too.

I emailed Barry Mayo about having Aaron on HOT 97 or KISS-FM. I pulled Sway aside and told him Aaron's story. He said his audience didn't want to hear about that kind of stuff. So I ended up bringing Aaron on my own show at KISS-FM. Although I was supposed to get clearance to have guests or deviate in any way from the playlist, I took a risk. How could I look at a man like Aaron, someone who had been wrongly imprisoned and later used six figures of his own money to bail someone out of jail, and not take some kind of action to help him?

As I brought him into the station, we ran into Funkmaster Flex. I asked Flex how many people he knew who had done time on death row. I introduced him to Aaron, and he gave Aaron a bear hug. I put Aaron on at about 10 p.m. that night, and the phone lines lit up and stayed lit for the entire show. People were calling in with questions for Aaron, questions about the legal system and stories of their own about police brutality and injustice.

About a week after I tried to get Aaron on HOT 97, I was tuning in to Sway's morning show and there were several prostitutes in the studio for a segment called "Do You Swallow?" I was disgusted. This was on when young people were getting ready for school. If this segment came on after hours, I wouldn't have said a word, but the subject matter wasn't appropriate for a morning drive show that earned advertising dollars marketing to young people.

I was appalled, because I knew that Sway would never consider doing a segment like that on MTV, where he delivered serious news and celebrity interviews. It seemed like he was doing a "good brother" shtick for the MTV crowd, showing them positive images of black men, while showing his ignorant ass on HOT 97. I stepped to him soon after the show and told him I thought it was inappropriate. He waved me off. I asked him if he would air the same segment on MTV. He said he would not. I asked, "Then why are you doing it here?" Sway told me I didn't know what was going on and that he was just giving the people what they wanted. I believed he was copying the shock style of Star and Buc Wild to try to keep up the ratings. He obviously did not respect the listeners enough to give them something better.

I couldn't stop thinking about Aaron Patterson and how Sway passed on having him on the show but welcomed prostitutes for a segment on swallowing semen. I wondered just how many HOT 97 listeners had dealt with dirty cops and a lopsided justice system. So they would listen to and embrace artists on a label called Death Row, but they wouldn't listen to a man who'd actually served time on death row for a crime he didn't commit? I wasn't buying it.

Aaron's life story was the personification of hip-hop music. He was a real-life version of what many of the rappers on radio pretended to be. But according to Sway, no one wanted to listen to Aaron. Sway was hiding behind the idea that the media just reflects the culture, which is bullshit. The media was shaping the culture. If Sway wanted to, he could have told his listeners that there was something important that he wanted to share, and they would have listened. He didn't realize the power he had to educate and inform. Or perhaps he just didn't care.

A few days after Sway's offensive morning show, I tuned in and heard Method Man on the show promoting his new album. He told Ebro, the Music Director, to play a track from the album. It was an unedited version full of profanity. They didn't stop the song halfway through or even say anything about it when the song ended. It was as if there were no rules about what could be played and when. I realized that I didn't even know the rules anymore. Nevertheless, I *did know* that the word "fuck" was not supposed to be heard on a morning show program. I went to the FCC website to file a complaint but only received an automated message that my complaint was received.

Sadly, HOT 97 was the leading hip-hop station in the country, and they heavily promoted the "dumbing down" of hip-hop culture. The jocks were raw and raunchy. Violence, misogyny, sex and all things vulgar and profane were aired 24 hours a day. There was no sunset for the vile conversations and music. Children were listening to toxic radio, and no one seemed to care.

Being back in New York with no real money coming in helped me to regain perspective. I was now taking public transportation to get around town. On the train, boomboxes blared gangsta rap while the DJs spoke garbled English, as if they'd never entered a formal classroom. Driving around the city, I'd hear hip hop full of curses and sex talk blasting from cars with young children inside. It was depressing, and even worse, it was endemic. These songs were planted seeds that would influence a cohort of black people, and no one would take responsibility. The jocks and artists just thought they were hip and in tune with what was happening in the streets. They were giving the people what they wanted and making money. Right? I was just an old man who was out of sync with the times.

The years were passing, and I was labeled as out of touch because I had the audacity to say that the children should not be exposed to rap's negative lyrics and images. I left KISS-FM in 2004, and soon after, I started thinking about launching a website to address issues of indecency. I began sowing the seeds for IndustryEars.com.

In 2004, when Janet Jackson's wardrobe malfunctioned during the Super Bowl halftime show, it seemed like the whole nation took offense. I kept hearing about how the FCC was going to levy fines for the indecent act. I thought about all the times I'd submitted complaints to the FCC when I was at KISS-FM and never got anything more than an automated response. I realized that although I had applied to the FCC for a broadcaster's license 20 years before, I had no idea what they were actually doing. I knew they were responsible for regulating indecency in radio and video, yet the indecency I'd repeatedly witnessed seemed to go unnoticed.

Commercial rap music was overrun with violent songs that objectified and degraded women. To make matters worse, the accompanying videos left nothing to the imagination. Half-naked young girls gyrated onscreen, and young girls on the street emulated their dress code and dance moves. I often thought about

106

Lea and other children who were growing up with these songs and this culture. Through commercial rap, young boys were learning to view females as sex objects, while young girls were led to believe that to "get the guy" they had to dress like strippers and embrace titles such as "bitch" or "hoe." Relationships, at least as they were modeled through mainstream rap, did not include romance, love or courting. But it seemed that no one saw this as a problem.

A few years prior, I had reconnected Lisa Fager. Lisa worked for Emmis Records and had lots of experience in the music industry. Over the years, she and I had talked repeatedly about what we could do make a positive difference. We didn't think that shock jocks should be silenced; rather, we felt that some balance and decency should be restored, and impressionable children should be shielded from negative lyrics and images. Lisa and I had many conversations about how misogynistic a lot of song lyrics had become and how radio was allowing the same degrading, violent, sexually explicit songs to be played with reckless abandon.

In 2004, little Lea asked me to help her get a song off the radio and, consequently, I left KISS-FM. This would be the beginning of my life's new mission. In 2005, in partnership with Lisa Fager, I launched IndustryEars.com, which had been on the back burner for many years. Our nonprofit, non-partisan, independent organization was formed to focus on the impact the media has on children in communities of color. From this experience, I would learn and then teach others about the role of government and how corporate decisions impact the music industry.

Chapter 9: Regulating the Industry

The idea for IndustryEars.com was conceived while I was still working as Program Director at BET. It was originally intended to be an online community for radio professionals, similar to what Urban Insite was doing in the late '90s. But

as I became more aware of how the content in the music was changing for the worse, and after my eye-opening encounter with young Lea at P.S. 192 in Queens, I switched my focus.

Too many times, people told me they had written letters and submitted complaints to the FCC about vile music and nasty videos with no results, just an automated acknowledgment that their complaint had been received. When people asked me what else they could do, I honestly didn't know what to tell them. It was clear that I needed to learn about the process so I could teach others.

I knew very little about government and politics, and I knew even less about running a think tank. But my co-founder, Lisa Fager, knew the recording industry, and I knew radio. We merged our collective experiences and began to fill in the knowledge gaps by researching and talking to people. It took more than a year for us to put together the content to officially launch IndustryEars.com, and one of our main targets was the FCC.

When most people think of the FCC, they probably think of Janet Jackson and Justin Timberlake's "Nipplegate" fiasco during the 2004 Super Bowl halftime show. The FCC was flooded with thousands of complaints the next day, and then-Chairman Michael Powell announced an investigation. Eventually, Viacom — parent company of MTV, which had produced the halftime show — paid out $3.5 million dollars in fines and penalties. While Janet Jackson's "wardrobe malfunction" was wholly inappropriate, if on that same day all the outraged parents who covered their children's eyes when her breast was exposed had turned off the television and turned on the radio instead, they might have been in for a bigger shock. The song "Get Low" by Lil Jon was getting lots of airplay that week, and most parents had no idea that this song with extremely offensive connotations was being marketed directly to their young children, or that, with the rise of gangsta rap, songs expressing themes of violence, murder, rape, and misogyny were in heavy rotation on hip-hop stations every day. This kind of content was going unnoticed by parents, and by the FCC. At IndustryEars.com, we dedicated our efforts to holding corporations accountable for this irresponsible content and getting the federal government to enforce the laws already on the books that pertained to obscenity, profanity, and indecency on the airwaves.

We began participating in lectures, campaigns, interviews and media appearances. We kicked off right in the middle HOT 97's Smackfest's fiasco, and our web site received more than 200,00 hits. By March 2005, I was on "Hannity & Colmes" discussing Smackfest, Rah Digga's "Party & Bullshit" and my departure from radio.

I was excited and relieved to get so much support. One night, as I surfed the Internet, I came across a press release about *Essence* magazine's "Take Back the Music" campaign to address the indecency in music. It wasn't about bashing the artists — it was about having some balance and awareness. I emailed Editor-in-Chief Diane Weathers, and she responded right away and invited me to the first town hall forum for the campaign. It was held on the Spelman College campus in February of 2005 with panelists Michael Llewellyn, a public relations executive from BET; Bryan Leach, a Vice President at TVT Records; writer and activist Kevin Powell and rapper MC Lyte.

The town hall forum drew a large crowd of participants that posed great questions about the negativity in Black music. The consensus was that as long as radio was playing degraded music, record labels would continue to make it in an effort to "give the people what they wanted to hear." It was all about supply and demand, and it was up to the public to demand something different from the industry.

At the forum, I was able to connect with some like-minded individuals, including Spelman student Moya Bailey. Moya had helped to organize a 2004 boycott of rapper Nelly in response to his sexually explicit video "Tip Drill," which appeared on "BET: Uncut" and featured the rapper pretending to swipe a credit card down a woman's butt crack in order to make her gyrate for him.

I was reminded of the time, soon after I'd left BET, when Stephen Hill approved "Uncut." Stephen originally said that "Uncut" would be an outlet for new artists, a chance for people to get on the air. But the truth behind the show was in its title. It was raw, over-sexualized and usually filled with videos that were made on the cheap. Most of these videos were not even shot digitally, which was then industry standard. It mostly became the dumping ground for all of the B-level artists who could never get any airtime on the station during the day. Most people who got their videos on that show were just happy to be on television and usually had no chance of making it any further in the business.

After the forum, Industry Ears continued to take steps to combat the negative images and messages in Black music. On September 25, 2007, representing Industry Ears, Lisa testified before the U.S. House of Representatives at the hearing "From Imus to Industry: The Business of Stereotypes and Degrading Images," focusing on the role media conglomerates play in perpetuating negative stereotypes. She testified that networks like Viacom made huge profits from airing content that demeaned women and people of color, particularly African-Americans. She also told Congress that payola was no longer the local disc jockey receiving money for airplay of a song; it was an organized corporate activity that supported a lack of balance, promoted degrading content and imagery primarily directed at women and African-Americans, excluded local and regional artists and resulted in the *same songs* being played over and over again.

The next big event for Industry Ears was the 2008 National Conference for Media Reform (NCMR) in Memphis, Tenn., which brought together more than 3,000 people. Speakers included journalist and political commentator Bill Moyers; actors and activists Jane Fonda, Geena Davis and Danny Glover; Civil Rights leaders Van Jones and Reverend Jesse Jackson; Senators Ed Markey and Bernie Sanders; and FCC Commissioners Michael Copps and Jonathan Adelstein.

At the conference, I represented Industry Ears on a panel exploring how payola occurs, why it continues and what it would take to stop it. I learned that the FCC — contrary to my beliefs as a young jock that the FCC was always hovering nearby, waiting for me to screw up so they could haul me off or fine me — *does not* have a staff of people that listens at random to the thousands of radio stations throughout this country; it only responds to complaints. So if no one complains about a song or show, the FCC takes no action, even if the song or show violates laws regarding obscenity, indecency, and profanity. I also learned that if only one person complains, the FCC most likely won't respond, but when an organization like the Parents Television Council (PTC) — a watchdog agency that monitors material on TV shows and works with government officials to enforce broadcast decency standards — sends 80,000 signatures attached to a complaint, the FCC reacts. In 2004, more than 80 percent of the complaints logged into the FCC came in through the PTC, which has more than 1.3 million members and 56 chapters across the United States. Since the FCC reacts to complaints by volume, you can be sure PTC complaints are handled more quickly.

In the ensuing years, we partnered with the PTC to get action on FCC complaints. Initially, it seemed strange to collaborate with a conservative organization, but we found that organizations like the NAACP and the Urban League were not willing to partner with us to file complaints against corporations that donated large sums of money to their organizations. It was also difficult to get popular DJs to support our efforts. Black churches and parents were our main supporters.

The PTC put up money and other resources to help us. Their analysts conducted a study titled "The Rap on Rap" to examine the degree to which adult-themed music videos were purposely marketed to and viewed by children, videotaping and analyzing every episode of MTV's "Sucker Free" and BET's "Rap City" and "106 & Park" programs.

The PTC's study found 1,342 instances of offensive adult content in the 14 hours of programming analyzed, an average of 95.8 instances per hour, or one instance of adult content every 38 seconds. By comparison, the FCC's analysis of prime-time, family-hour programming during this same period revealed an average of 12.5 instances per hour of violence, profanity and sexual content, or one instance every 4.8 minutes. Sex represented the majority of adult content in rap music videos, followed by explicit language, violence, drug use or sales, and other illegal activity.

The study also found that Procter & Gamble was the top advertiser on all three shows it surveyed, with a total of 78 ads within 27.5 hours of programming, and revealed that more than 85 percent of the music promoted on the three shows was sponsored by two record labels — Universal Music and Warner Music.

Organizations like the PTC have to take up the cause to move the FCC toward responsible action, because there simply aren't enough federal dollars allocated to investigate individual complaints, and the FCC's legalese can be quite deceiving. They sound like an agency that gets things done, but we quickly learned that their content enforcement was mostly smoke and mirrors. At the time, the FCC had only two investigators for the entire USA that dealt with content; the majority of FCC employees handled matters involving licensing and telecommunications.

My experience with young Lea in Queens made me wonder about the FCC and what they were actually doing. I also started to pay closer attention to what was being played on the radio. I discovered that there were lots of tracks on the radio that made Rah Digga's "Party & Bullshit" sound like a nursery rhyme. Use any search engine and look up the lyrics to songs like "Get Low" by Lil' Jon and the East Side Boyz, "Play" by David Banner, "Some Cut" by Trillville and "Wait" by the Ying Yang Twins. The lightly edited versions of these lewd, misogynistic songs were in heavy rotation on stations across the country. These songs didn't just slyly mention physical relationships with women; they bragged about defiling women and talked about women in ways that are degrading, disrespectful, and even illegal.

Industry Ears filed complaints with the FCC about the four songs listed above on more than 15 different occasions, and through a form on IndustryEars.com, there have been nearly 150 complaints filed, but we rarely received any response besides an automated email reply.

The FCC has made some changes over the years. As of this writing, the FCC has assigned more staff to enforce indecency laws; the enforcement branch now has 17 attorneys and 16 other support personnel that work on matters involving obscenity, indecency and profanity, up from just two a few years ago. You can now file a complaint using an online complaint form or by calling the FCC, and your call should not go directly to a voicemail graveyard. Concerned citizens now have numerous ways to contact this agency, and I hope they will use them.

Through the collective efforts of the PTC, Industry Ears and the 2007 "Enough is Enough" campaign that protested the marketing of derogatory images of black men and women in the entertainment industry, an increasing number of people became fed up with sexually explicit, violent, degrading music that reinforced negative black stereotypes. While Industry Ears had its fair share of successes, Lisa and I became disillusioned. Industry Ears got a lot of press, but we did not end up helping the masses of young people who were still being subjected to negative messages and images. We decided to part ways and move on to other projects. In 2010, I continued to work on Industry Ears by myself as I began to think about focusing more on young voices, popular culture, and helping artists navigate their way through the music industry. The seeds for a new business model, which would soon become Rap Rehab, were being planted in my mind.

Chapter 10: Corporate Decisions

I decided to form Rap Rehab as a limited liability company (LLC); I figured there would be no more restrictive, nonprofit rules for me to follow. I've always been opinionated and outspoken, and I didn't want to start another business where my hands would be tied and my mouth would be forced shut by the complicated guidelines of a nonprofit structure. It wasn't going to go down like that with Rap Rehab. I would have an independent voice.

While trying to set up Rap Rehab, I thought a lot about what consolidation had done to the radio industry in the USA. I saw corporations growing fatter, while the quality of the radio experience declined. Radio stations no longer had their own unique identities, and they no longer served the local community. Computer-generated voice segments were played to make listeners think that a program was being broadcast exclusively for their locality. But in reality, that same program was being aired in multiple cities across the USA from one central location, with one person simultaneously playing the appropriate pre-recorded greetings to match the locale: *Hello, DC!* or *What's up, Atlanta?* or *Yo, what's happening, New York!* after airing the same songs across the airwaves.

This was all the result of the Telecommunications Act of 1996 (TCA), which removed restrictions regarding the number of radio stations a single entity could own. While the TCA was designed to promote greater competition for big communication companies that monopolized the market, it actually had the opposite effect and led to massive media consolidation. Before the ink was dry on the bill, companies like Clear Channel went on a buying spree. The price for a radio station went through the roof, and as large companies bought stations, you would have had to be one of Forbes' billionaires to afford a commercial radio station. Mom and Pop-owned radio stations were becoming a thing of the past as they quickly sold to large corporations. There were fewer individual owners and fewer people willing and able to take a stand against them. Somehow, a provision that sought to eliminate monopolies actually helped to create them.

Before long, seven companies owned 70% of the radio stations in the United States. That meant smaller, corporate-influenced radio playlists and "radio homogenization," a term used to describe programming that's the same across different formats. Creativity, individuality and hometown connections were not a part of the formula in the new one-size-fits-all approach. Syndicated formats muted local news, alternative voices and opinions, eliminated regional sounds and played the same songs over and over. Diversity died as large, faceless corporations decided what music would be heard on the airwaves, pushing negative messages into the mainstream that dumb down our kids. Meanwhile, payola increased, making it difficult for artists who were not backed by major labels to get airplay.

Of course, black listeners were the guinea pigs. One finding indicated that black people are 75 times more likely to hear syndicated programming than white people, and Black radio is syndicated more than any other music-based format in the country. Black radio had turned into a corporate machine, pumping out pre-approved playlists of corporate-selected songs. Out went local talent, music and public service; in came condensed playlists and cost-cutting measures like hiring inexperienced jocks to benefit stockholders. We've gone from hearing insightful stories written by great lyricists to being forced-fed the inane garbled lingo of the lyrically challenged.

In the shadow of all these changes, Rap Rehab was launched on January 15, 2010, Martin Luther King Jr.'s birthday. Rap Rehab aims to speak the truth about an industry that is dominated by a few major corporations. The USA does a great job of projecting an image of a free press, but a closer look at the numbers reveals the opposite. By 2011, there were six corporations — CBS, Disney, GE, News Corp, Time Warner and Viacom — that controlled 90 percent of media in the country. In 2011, the combined total revenue for these six corporations was $275.9 billion, with 232 media executives controlling the flow of information for 277 million people in the U.S. This included 1,500 newspapers, 1,100 magazines, 9,000 radio stations 1,500 TV stations and 2,400 publishing companies owned by these corporations.

I wanted to put a more critical eye on what was happening in the music industry, with a focus on developing new artists and monitoring corporate decisions that impacted music. I wanted less involvement with government and more involvement with young people interested in learning about the music industry.

In June 2011, I joined in with the PTC and the "Enough Is Enough" campaign to ask Viacom, which purchased BET in 2001, to stop airing Rihanna's "Man Down" music video, which featured a graphic portrayal of Rihanna getting back at a violent attacker by shooting him in a crowded train station and then leaving the scene of the crime. In response to the controversy, Rihanna tweeted to her fans that her video had a "very strong underlying message 4 girls like me!" She thanked her fans for their support and facetiously thanked us for helping to promote her record. My concern was not directed at Rihanna's so-called "creative expression." I felt she could have told her story and expressed herself without blowing the man's head off in a video that she knew would be shown to young people all around the world. My outrage, however, was directed at Viacom/BET for exploiting the situation and providing a platform for the video to be shown to a young, impressionable audience in the middle of the afternoon.

This was not my first time speaking out against Rihanna's "artistic" expression. In 2009, she released "Russian Roulette," a song with lyrics that seemed to promote suicide: *"Know that I must pass the test. So just pull the trigger."* I appeared on "Entertainment Tonight" representing Industry Ears to oppose the industry green lighting the song. It was an R-rated album with a song marketed to a young audience. My position was clear: Record companies, radio stations and TV stations need to be held accountable for the material they broadcast to young people.

***

I had relocated to Florida to help take care of my ailing mother. She made her transition on January 3, 2012, and it was an extremely rough year for me. The beauty of life, however, is that many family members and friends reached out to me with expressions of love and sympathy. The strong outpouring of support and encouragement propelled me to move forward, despite the fact that I had lost my beloved mother. I knew she would not be happy seeing me curled up in a ball of sadness and depression. So, slowly but deliberately, I begin to get back to work. There was so much going on in the music industry, and I needed to stay busy and focused.

A few months after my mother's passing, a seed of opportunity was planted by Paul Billings of Muskegon, Mich. I'd known Paul for several years and had been a frequent guest on his Low Power FM (LPFM) radio station, WUVS 103.7, The Beat, to discuss issues in the music industry. Paul came down to Florida to attend my mother's funeral service, and I was surprised to see him and grateful for his support. The next time we talked, he told me there was a signal in Orlando and asked if I would be interested in applying to the FCC for it. It was an opportunity for me to own a local community radio station. Of course I was interested. I was excited, too. Paul Billings, the guru of LPFM, was willing to collaborate with me and walk me through the process. We had no idea at the time that it would be a five-year walk before the station was launched. Nevertheless, for me, it was worth every step.

Meanwhile, in the quest to gain "street credibility" and appeal to the young urban segment of the market, corporate decisions were being made that were controversial and irresponsible. In April of 2012, Reebok hired Rick Ross as a spokesperson for the brand. Controversy erupted when Ross appeared to allude to date raping a woman using the drug Molly — the street name for MDMA, the active ingredient in Ecstasy — in Rocko's 2013 song,

"U.O.E.N.O.": *"Put Molly all in her champagne, she ain't even know it/I took her home and I enjoyed that, she ain't even know it."* Rap Rehab joined in with Ultra Violet, a women's rights advocacy group that initiated a petition of protest, and other individuals and organizations to demand that Reebok drop Ross as a spokesman. More than 72,000 signatures were delivered to Reebok denouncing Ross' lyrics that appeared to condone date rape and suggested a blatant disregard for women.

By April 2013, Ross' contract with Reebok was terminated. In conjunction with Ultra Violet's petition, our coalition of concerned men, women, parents, advertisers, stockholders. and consumers demanded responsibility from the broadcast and recording industry. Ross apologized for his lyrics, claiming they were not about rape, and Rocko later dropped the Rick Ross verse in the song order to get radio play.

Reebok was not the only corporation to hire and fire a major rapper. In 2013, PepsiCo was embroiled in a major controversy after hiring Lil Wayne to be the spokesperson for Mountain Dew without knowing much about his content. In 2013, Wayne rapped on Future's song "Karate Chop": *"Bout to put rims on my skateboard wheels/Beat that pussy up like Emmett Till,"* an ignorant and wildly insensitive reference to the teen who was brutally lynched in Mississippi in 1955 after being falsely accused of flirting with a white woman. Wayne's disrespectful lyrics caused an uproar, and the family and estate of Emmett Till released a statement of disapproval over them.

Frank Cooper, a senior executive for PepsiCo, was an old associate of mine who had hired me to work as a music consultant for AOL back in 2008. I asked Frank, "How much research did you do?" Of course, no one had officially analyzed the implications of courting Lil Wayne. Over the next three days, I coached Frank through the process of damage control. I appeared on CNN twice and wrote articles to protect PepsiCo and Frank Cooper. That same week, PepsiCo dumped Lil Wayne. The rapper pledged to never perform the lyrics from "Karate Chop" again.

After Reverend Al Sharpton saw me on CNN, I heard that he contacted Frank Cooper asking, "Who is this Paul Porter guy?" Sharpton wanted to take the lead in working with Lil Wayne and the Till family. Frank dropped me like a hot potato after I had done most of the heavy lifting for him and his company. In the end, PepsiCo and the Till family paid money to Al Sharpton, who was supposed to do damage control. A meeting was held on May 8 with the Till family, but Lil Wayne did not attend. The Tills got a pseudo-apology from Lil Wayne, which they rejected. Rev. Sharpton issued a public statement calling the incident a "teaching moment" for all concerned. By July 2013, there was a press announcement of Reverend Sharpton's new $5 million dollar book deal with Lil Wayne's Cash Money Content, the publishing arm of Cash Money Records. Sharpton promised to get rappers to tone down their lyrics. Instead, the Reverend got paid from every angle and went on his way to chase the next ambulance.

Some folks wanted to know why Rap Rehab went after Lil Wayne and Rick Ross when there are scores of rappers spouting reprehensible lyrics. I thought it a fair question with a fair answer: No one knows who those rappers are, and therefore, their stories would never get the attention of the media and the public. Whenever you highlight the lyrics or images of a popular star, the issue generates publicity and starts a conversation with parents who see their kids bobbing their heads to the music but have no idea what the records are saying. After a big story hits the news, parents and educators race to the Internet to print the lyric sheet and grab an urban dictionary. Once they understand the messages that are being conveyed to their children, they voice their dissent and join the campaign to get the video or song pulled off the air.

Sometimes these collective efforts result in a major rapper or singer losing major endorsements. If an artist loses a million-dollar contract over a bad verse, or if record sales decline, potential violators take notice and pause. I watch the numbers closely, and I can say with assurance that sales decline after protests are lodged. For me, the bottom line is this: If Rap Rehab is able to educate the public — especially parents of young children — about inappropriate lyrics and images in music and hold corporations accountable for this negative content, then we have done our job.

Back in my office at Rap Rehab, I was doing all I could to provide valuable information about the music industry for fans, parents, and artists in need of guidance. Initially, I worked with a webmaster, but now I do most of the web and mobile content management myself. Sometimes I am a one-man show, editing, reading and researching. We have a wide selection of articles, from commentary on music, life, and culture to resources for aspiring artists on everything from writing press releases to understanding 360 deals. The most popular article on the site, "How to Destroy a Black Male in 10 Steps" by Andre G, a freelance writer, music producer and co-founder of ColorTheFuture.org, has been shared more than 65,000 times.

I work closely with a few valued contributors who are knowledgeable about the business, plus they're great writers: Lauren Carter is a writer and editor based in the Boston area; Sebastien (Seb) Elkouby, who has been working with me since 2010, is a hip-hop historian, freelance writer, consultant, and award-winning educator; and Camille H is a writer editor, educator, and public speaker with a Master's in Urban Affairs. These writers have become an essential part of my team, and their articles have been circulated widely. We do have other great writers who allow me to post their articles free of charge, but that is rare. Most established writers want to charge a fee up front. I don't blame them; I just can't afford to pay them. I am fortunate to have industry experts, artists, activists, and friends who provide resources to Rap Rehab. When I first started out, I caught a lot of heat. Now, some of my former critics are partnering with me. All Def Digital, Russell Simmons' digital company, teamed up with Rap Rehab and now converts some of our stories into videos.

In 2015, 3.5 million people visited Rap Rehab, mainly from Twitter and Facebook, and analytics reveal that we have fans around the world, from London to Saudi Arabia to Brazil. Rap

Rehab is building up its Internet game, and it's an honor to be recognized worldwide. My focus, however, is to take care of home first.

After extensive engineering studies, FCC procrastination and other start-up costs, WHPB, The WIRE 98.5 FM, hit the airwaves on October 28, 2016, to serve the community of Pine Hills located near metro Orlando, the #33 radio market in the U.S. The WIRE was one of just 2,000 FM stations across the country that received new licenses from the FCC in the last two years. The FCC's only requirement was that the applicants be nonprofit organizations committed to broadcasting locally originating programs.

The WIRE is a full-service community station that plays hip hop and R&B music, fills the void with conscious talk, and gives residents of Pine Hills and Metro Orlando a much-needed voice that reflects their concerns. It is live streamed at TheWire985.com, with listeners from as far away as Japan, but we are dedicated to serving the local community. On our launch day, we were fortunate to have some well-known guests, including Joy-Ann Reid of MSNBC; James Brown of CBS Sports; filmmaker Byron Hurt; and my former boss, BET and radio icon Donnie Simpson.

With Rap Rehab and The WIRE, I felt as though all my years of hard work were paying off. I now had two vehicles to make contributions to music, youth, and popular culture. Rap Rehab was an industry leader, and Black radio now had another positive signal with The WIRE 98.5. I felt as though "Captain" Paul Porter was embarking on one of the most meaningful journeys in his life.

Chapter 11: Music, Media and Modern Youth Culture

I chose the name "The WIRE" because it symbolizes energy, information and power — positive energy, information and power. That's what up! Those are the attributes that this so-called "majority-minority" community of about 60,000 desperately needs.

The WIRE is based in Pine Hills, a subdivision located west of Orlando. Disparagingly known as "Crime Hill," Pine Hills has one of the highest murder rates in the United States. But it wasn't always that way. In the city's early days, Pine Hills was an upper-middle class suburb with a country club named "Silver Pines." What happened to Pine Hills is the same thing that happened to Baltimore, Detroit, Richmond and "fill in the city": Big business moved out and took the jobs with them. No jobs equal no money, yielding increased poverty, an increased reliance on government assistance and a proliferation of crime.

Pine Hills is no longer affluent. Apartment buildings sprung up on the property where the Silver Pines Country Club once stood. The Pine Hills Shopping Center is now a discount mall. Large segments of the population live in rental and government-subsidized housing. This decay in living standards has existed for more than 20 years. Crime began to increase in Pine Hills in the late '80s, and local law enforcement and media coined the nickname "Crime Hill" when referring to the area. Sadly, the nickname caught on, and folks in the community started using Crime Hill to identify where they live.

Pine Hills has a large black and multicultural (Puerto Rican, Jamaican and Haitian) population. Music-wise, many of its young citizens are connected with hip-hop culture. The music produced by Pine Hills rappers is primarily gangsta rap, and the lyrics convey much of what's happening in the area. It's definitely not music made to lift your mood.

The WIRE is located on Silver Star Road in the center of most of the despair. Within the first eight weeks of starting the radio station, there were 12 murders in Pine Hills. The victims included a pregnant woman and a female police officer, both killed by a 41-year-old man whose life ambition, according to his Facebook page, is to be featured on "America's Most Wanted." I've started carrying a bigger gun, and I've replaced my nine-bullet gun with a 14-bullet gun, hoping that I will never have to use any bullets for any reason.

Nonetheless, there is good news in Pine Hills, and I intend to highlight it. Commercial media will continue to visit Pine Hills to feature the murder stories and the blight. "If it bleeds, it leads," is their mentality. While The WIRE does report on the murders and other crimes, we also emphasize the upstanding citizens, the young people engaged in constructive endeavors and the positive happenings in the area. We aim to provide some balance.

I've been juggling running Rap Rehab along with managing programming, sales, marketing, production and more at the WIRE. Needless to say, I am quickly learning to delegate. In my first few weeks in Pine Hills, I met a young brother who seems destined for greatness. Justin Fortune is a 19-year-old who manages a Facebook blog called "Pine Hill Talks." We interviewed Justin on The WIRE and found that he feels the heartbeat of the community. When Master Sergeant Debra Clayton, a 17-veteran of the police force, was murdered and Deputy Norm Lewis was killed in a motorcycle crash while in pursuit of her killer, Justin helped to organize a candlelight vigil to honor the officers who had worked with youth in the community.

I gave Justin a job at The WIRE as Director of Social Media. Straight away, he was busy posting stories and news, and I am delighted to have him on the team. Miles Murain, another young leader in Pine Hills who has a nonprofit called "Let Your Voice Be Heard," has been helpful in connecting folks at The WIRE with youth in the community. Miles is defying the negative stereotypes waged against dark-skinned black men with long dreadlocks. He is an activist who works with high school students in the community and has a lot of ambition. Miles was also interviewed on The WIRE, and he was featured on the local news for his leadership in planning the candlelight vigil.

At The WIRE, we play conscious hip hop that attracts a young audience. As much as I love the old school music of my generation, I don't want to be out of touch with young listeners, a mistake Cathy Hughes made when I started working at Majic. On The WIRE, we do play a little old school, but not much, and there is no fragmentation. In the same set, we might play a song by Gil Scott Heron — the original rapper — and follow that with a song by Drake. Our listeners dig it.

Every Saturday at noon, Camille H and Sebastien (Seb) Elkouby host a talk show called "Take No Prisoners Radio," which offers real talk about hip-hop culture and social justice. TNPR doesn't hold back when it comes to tackling issues related to the music industry, including racism, corrupt politicians and wack rappers. If it's a hot topic in the news or on social media, then Camille and Seb are probably talking about it on TNPR! And, in the midst of all the thought–provoking conversation, conscious hip-hop music promoting Black pride, self-determination, faith, peace, empowerment, cooperative economics and spirituality is played.

We've started to feature Rap Rehab stories in TNPR interviews and invite writers onto the show, including the author of a popular Rap Rehab article titled "Confessions of a Black Misogynistic Male." I believe that connecting Rap Rehab and The WIRE will benefit the community, especially the youth. The two missions are intertwined, and so far, it's been a great partnership.

At The WIRE, we aim to dispel the negative stereotypes lodged against black, brown and poor youth. We also wish to restore a sense of community and unity, and to help usher in the rebirth of Black radio.

Historically, Black radio was the one place where people of color could find positive messages. We learned to be "Black and Proud" by listening to James Brown, Curtis Mayfield, Gil Scott Heron and Marvin Gaye. We knew we needed to raise our awareness when Harold Melvin and the Blue Notes sang "Wake Up Everybody." We knew we were smart and worthy and talented when Donny Hathaway sang "To Be Young, Gifted and Black." The music helped to articulate our experiences and shape our values, with powerful messages that often propelled us to action and sparked movements. Black commentators were an important part of the communities that their stations were licensed to serve, and Black radio's mixture of news and music was an integral part of black culture. Black radio rarely used to miss spotlighting local issues; it was the rock of the culture.

But consolidation ended an era of positivity and diversity nearly 20 years ago. Gone are the days of R&B super groups like The Commodores, Earth, Wind & Fire, The Isley Brothers, LTD, Maze, and Sly & The Family Stone or conscious, empowering hip-hop artists like KRS-One, Public Enemy, A Tribe Called Quest or Lauryn Hill. They've been systematically replaced with samples and misogynistic hip hop, while Black radio hosts, once plugged in to the community, have become minions for the corporate music industry. Now, Black radio merely looks and sounds Black; in reality, it represents corporate interests, not community ones.

I'll give Black radio credit for backing President Obama's campaigns, Black Lives Matter and Jena 6, and for being out front on the murders of Trayvon Martin, Sandra Bland and other high-profile cases. I was excited that radio stations around the country stopped the music to host town halls and discuss real-life issues on live broadcasts. But after all the conscious talk, what's the final message to listener when Black radio consistently plays music filled with negative messages and stereotypes?

One morning, I got a call from a close friend who had tuned in to Radio One's syndicated morning show hosted by Rickey Smiley. Smiley was on a rant explaining why he was sick and tired of the media distorting the efforts of the Black Lives Matter movement. After his rant, Smiley immediately played a song filled with lyrics about drugs, sex, violence, misogyny and criminal activity. The lyrics obliterated every positive thing that Smiley had just said. My friend said he wondered how Smiley could end a message about the media distorting images of black people by playing a song that distorts images of black people. The words "hypocritical" and "irresponsible" came to my mind.

I would never argue that commercial rap music is responsible for all of the problems associated with modern-day youth culture, but I believe it is a major contributor. Just as a magnet attracts and rearranges material within its field, music affects and influences youth culture. It always has, and it always will. The difference is that today, we "mainstream" music with negative themes and marginalize music with positive messages, when we could be exposing our youth to conscious music that uplifts and inspires greatness. Popular rap music has changed from being meaningful and inspirational to being a sensational, decadent force that hurts the black community and lines corporate executives' pockets. Our youth — more vulnerable to the influences of music and media because they're still developing cognitively, emotionally, and spiritually — are on a steady diet of bitch, hoe, and bling.

That's why I support public and LPFM radio as an alternative to commercial stations. I believe that radio must reaffirm its commitment to serving the communities in which it holds licenses; it needs to think, program, and act locally. In this way, we might rebuild the vital connections between listeners, artists, labels, and programmers so everyone can benefit from the public airwaves. Locally-owned and operated radio stations can do great things. Black radio needs to lead by example. Conscious content is out there, and we need to hear lyrics that uplift the people, now more than ever. It is time to repeat history. With The WIRE, that's exactly what we're aiming to do.

Chapter 12: Lessons Learned

Listening to music can be invigorating. During my formative years, there was a heavy emphasis on songs with uplifting beats and lyrics. While there have always been — and will always be — raunchy songs replete with sexual innuendos and tales of the depraved, as young children we were not routinely exposed to them. We had adult supervision and balance in our musical selections. Even when we secretly heard adult-themed songs, we rarely understood the meaning, and we certainly weren't going to risk getting a butt whipping by asking an adult to interpret the lyrics. Furthermore, there were no video images to make the songs' intent graphically clear. There was a large selection of music advocating themes of romance, peace, and happiness. I realize now that those songs made a positive difference in our lives.

I have always known the importance of working with others to help inspire a brother, a sister or a neighbor. My outlook on life was shaped by growing up in Jamaica, Queens in a "village setting," and then moving on to Northeastern University, where most of the black students supported each other as an extended family. I grew up knowing that people could thrive by working collectively to build each other up. Our focus was not on what we didn't have; rather, we focused on sharing our resources, no matter how scarce, and encouraging each other to succeed. I have carried this ethos with me throughout my life.

In 2009, when I attended the National Association of Broadcasters conference in Tampa, Fla., I ran into Stan Verrett, a former colleague who is now an anchorman on ESPN. Stan reminded me that I hired him for a job at Majic back in 1988. At the time, he was paid $10 an hour, and I used to give him extra to double his pay. I also talked to Darius Walker who was, at the time, New York Bureau Chief for CNN. I first met Darius when he ran track at Northeastern University. Darius recalled how I recruited him to do the news for me at WRBB. He said that experience put him on the path to a career in communications. Similar acts of encouragement and support have been afforded to me over the years. Up until the time I worked for Cathy Hughes, I had never met a black person who took advantage of other people to get ahead. I trusted Cathy because I thought she was a "sister." I rolled up my sleeves to help her build Majic, because I thought that if she succeeded, she would do right by me and the rest of her employees.

I looked up to Cathy Hughes, and her AM station WOL was a strong voice for the people in Washington, D.C. But once she started making money, her true personality was revealed. I could certainly understand her desire to make money, but I will never understand why she wasn't willing to adequately compensate employees who contributed to her financial success. Nonetheless, I am glad for the experience of working for Cathy Hughes at Majic, because I learned a lot. The experience cemented the wise advice that Imhotep Gary Byrd gave his listening audience in my early years of tuning in to his radio talks: *"Every brother ain't a brother, and every sister ain't a sister."*

There's a lot of money changing hands these days, with no true commitment to dig down deep and do some hands-on damage repair in our blighted communities. I still remember Barry Mayo boasting to me about how much money he gave to the 'hood when I met with him to talk about the songs they were playing on HOT 97. I wondered: If Barry really believed that the music on HOT 97 was acceptable, why was he telling me that he gave money to the communities that were targeted by negative music? His boast suggested to me that while in pursuit of money and power, Barry recognized his participation in damaging modern youth culture.

People want to make money. I get it. So do I. But if you're not doing anything to help someone else, if you're making money by creating or promoting a product that harms others, are you really successful? Life has proven to me that a person making $15,000 a year who helps to lift up 50 people is more successful and has more power and self-respect than a person making $500,000 dollars a year who helps no one but themselves and only has a big house, fancy cars and an expensive lifestyle to display. I once fell victim to a materialistic mentality, but never at the expense of brazenly exposing someone else's child to something I would not want for my own children, or by cheating other people out of a living wage. At the end of the day, self-serving behavior makes for an empty life.

I've associated with lots of people with plenty of money and assets, and I have learned that life is not made secure by what you possess, even when you have much more than you need. To me, life is made secure by taking care of your soul and not selling out to the highest bidder. Life is made secure by helping others and sharing resources. As I said before, there is nothing wrong with having lots of money, but we'd be wise to remember that not everything is about material possessions and financial gain. These are the words of a poor man who has been granted many opportunities to sell out. I am satisfied with my choice to remain true to my values. If fortune ever comes knocking at my door again, I will know that I earned it with integrity.

I am far from perfect. Often, I have to check myself to ensure that I am not taking a hypocritical stance by pointing a finger at others for things I am guilty of. I've learned that I just need to continue working to tear back the veil to expose what is happening to our communities and to our children as a result of syndication, payola, fake leaders, and the same foul messages and songs. I am willing to work with anyone who is willing to work with me to share resources, promote positive alternatives in music and media, and provide constructive opportunities for our youth. I am dedicated to achieving results. It is my desire to make a positive difference.

Where is this world going? I do not know. What will it take to restore a sense of pride and unity in our local communities? I have a few ideas. With certainty, I know there is not much the government can or will do. We the people are the ones with the power and the potential to change our situation.

There is much hard work to be done to improve the human condition, especially in majority-minority communities, but I believe in our collective power to make the necessary positive moves. There are many areas for improvement, but what I know well is music. I know it can be a catalyst for the restoration of values, traditions, and mores that are the hallmarks of our greatness. It's about our choices in lyrics. It's about balance. Music influences our children's behavior, thoughts, and desires. One song can change a child's life for better or worse. These are our future leaders, and we need to pay attention to the messages that are being planted in their minds, because in time those messages will help to shape their thoughts, values , and behaviors, and determine what kind of mark they will leave on this world.

If a young boy keeps hearing the same stories and songs about the uncle in jail and the brother who sells drugs and the women who are sex objects, who do you think he will become? For young girls, the same logic applies. How do you think girls are made to feel when a teen idol like Chris Brown refers to women as hoes who are only in it for the money, as in his song, "Loyal?"

Unfortunately, children will continue to be offered the same offensive songs and the same degrading videos unless we put a stop to it or provide an alternative. Things won't change for the better until we demand something else. In the words of Frederick Douglass, "Power concedes nothing without a demand." That's why it's important to support college stations and nonprofit radio stations like The WIRE in Pine Hills, Fla., and The Beat in Muskegon, Mich., as well as other local stations that feature music by artists who can articulate the complexity of our identity and our struggle.

Yes, it can get frustrating when challenging the promotion of offensive music to young kids, but I have seen promising changes over the years. More and more people contact me to talk about the music and its negative impact on children. They are no longer trying to drown out everything that I say. They want to ask questions, join in and help advance the cause. Young and old folks are speaking out. Even some of the rappers who have grown up in the business are publicly announcing their concerns regarding offensive, disrespectful, and ridiculous lyrics.

Back when my good friend Jay Dixon was working at KISS-FM in New York, he advised me many times, "Paul, man, you gotta be more corporate and play the game." I was never interested in playing the game. It seemed to me that people who played the game were not provided opportunities to be creative and had to stifle their true thoughts. They had to toe the line. Playing the game meant kissing ass to climb the ladder. I've never been interested in that path to success.

Thinking about that conversation with Jay caused me reflect on what had become of many of the people I started out in the game with. Jay Dixon is now a consultant at HOT 97 and WBLS in New York. My friend Harold Austin, with whom I used to throw the HAPPY parties in Boston, worked as an actor and manages several properties in Boston. Earl Boston, who taught me how to use Selector and warned me many years ago that computers were the future, is now considered an expert in Selector and is the owner of his own company, helping programmers across the country.

My friend Candy Shannon, who I worked with at WKYS, is an Associate Professor at Howard University's School of Communications. She hosts and produces "The Morning Brew – Friday Edition" on WPFW-89.3 FM in Washington, D.C. My friend Jeff Leonard from WKYS retired from radio and television and does voice-overs and commercials for radio and television. Donnie Simpson, my first connection to the big time in radio, the man who gave me the corny "Captain" nickname that stuck, came out of a five-year retirement to host the "Donnie Simpson Show" on Majic and "Donnie After Dark" on TV One.

Alfred Liggins III is the Chief Executive Officer and President of Radio One, and his mother, Cathy Hughes, is Chairperson and Founder of Radio One and a minority owner of BET industries. In October 2016, Liggins reportedly donated $4 million dollars to Howard University. That same month, the Howard University

School of Communications was renamed Cathy Hughes School of Communications.

Lee Michaels hosts an Internet radio show in Los Angeles, Calif. Debra Lee is Chairman and Chief Executive Officer of BET. Steve Crumbley is Program Director at Apex Broadcasting in South Carolina. Stephen Hill recently stepped down from his position as President of Programming at BET.

My friend Tim Winter, who brought me on the board of the Parents Television Council and has been a major supporter of Industry Ears and Rap Rehab, is President of the PTC. My partner at Industry Ears, Lisa Fager, is Director of Public Policy and Solutions at Hip-Hop Caucus.

My great mentor, Sunny Joe White, passed away in 1996. At that time, I was flat broke and had no way to get to Boston for the services, but I had to be there. Jay Dixon, Earl Boston and I rented a car and drove up together to the memorial service. Sunny Joe helped countless people of all races in the radio industry, so I was shocked to witness how very few people were in attendance to pay their final respects to this most generous and talented man. Being at Sunny Joe's service reminded me that there are people who act nice because they want access to something you can give them, but when you are down and out, they will forget you ever existed.

In 2000, the great Frankie Crocker died in Miami, Fla. His was a tragic story of a successful man who lived most of his life surrounded by the crowd, but died alone. Mercyline "Mike" Bernardo, the record executive who sent two boxes of records to WRBB with 100 albums inside, and who helped me get a job with Sylvia Rhone, died in 2012. I don't know what happened to Cindy Mahmoud, but I appreciate all she did to help my career. Sylvia Rhone is President of Epic Records.

Forty years have passed since I first ventured off to Northeastern University in Boston to join the student-run radio station WRBB. My love-struck decision to follow JoAnn to Boston put me on a path that opened up countless opportunities for me in the entertainment industry and changed my life. Years later, taking action on the note Lea handed me outside of P.S. 192 put me on a different path. Lea's message became the catalyst that shifted me from commercial radio to unemployment, to teaching, to talk radio, to Industry Ears, and then, to Rap Rehab and The WIRE. I do not regret my decision to dedicate my life's efforts to challenging the violent, degrading, misogynistic and offensive music that has been promoted to destroy our culture and, by extension, our children.

With Rap Rehab and The WIRE going strong, I feel as though I am in a great place. I have done everything I set out to do and more. I am grateful. I work with a dedicated group of people, and I have a strong professional network. I am still connected to my best childhood friends, Lynn, Bucky, and Renny. My sons, Miles and Xavier, are doing well. Sadly, my father transitioned in 1996, but years later, I was blessed to reconnect with my half-sister Elizabeth, who I'd lost contact with for several years. She and her husband Todd are the parents of my adorable twin nephews, Porter and Alexander. My dog Diva is my best friend ever. I have little money, and I face many challenges, but all of my needs are met. One of my "village mothers," Mrs. Staton, transitioned in 2016. I will forever miss her, as I will miss my mother, who made her transition in 2012. I find strength in knowing they are resting in "heavenly peace."

Whenever I am down, I just force myself to get back up. I just keep fighting harder. I have seen most of it before. Thus far, I have survived. I used to wonder what would have happened if I had chosen to ignore the message Lea handed me, or if after receiving the ultimatum from Barry Mayo, I'd decided to be compliant. I no longer question those decisions. I shudder to think that if I had acted any other way, I would be hunched over in somebody's dank radio station, having no self-respect, just playing the same old tired songs.

I am proud!

CPSIA information can be obtained
at www.ICGtesting.com
Printed in the USA
BVOW06s0038011017
496081BV00010BE/310/P